D1489166

FOCUS
AND FINISH

ZACH ERTZ

HARVEST HOUSE PUBLISHERS
EUGENE, OREGON

All Scripture quotations are from The ESV® Bible (The Holy Bible, English Standard Version®), copyright © 2001 by Crossway, a publishing ministry of Good News Publishers. Used by permission. All rights reserved.

Cover photos of Zach Ertz by Tom DiPace © 2019

Front cover texture © Aerial3 / Getty Images

Cover design by Kyler Dougherty

Interior design by KUHN Design Group

HARVEST KIDS is a trademark of The Hawkins Children's LLC. Harvest House Publishers, Inc., is the exclusive licensee of the trademark HARVEST KIDS.

Focus and Finish
Published by Harvest House Publishers
Eugene, Oregon 97408
www.harvesthousepublishers.com

ISBN 978-0-7369-7930-6 (hardcover)
ISBN 978-0-7369-7931-3 (eBook)

Library of Congress Cataloging-in-Publication Data

Names: Ertz, Zach, 1990- author.
Title: Focus and finish / Zach Ertz.
Description: Eugene, Oregon : Harvest House Publishers, [2019] | Audience:
   Ages: 8-12.
Identifiers: LCCN 2019017563 (print) | LCCN 2019021891 (ebook) | ISBN
   9780736979313 (ebook) | ISBN 9780736979306 (hardcover) | ISBN
   9780736979313 (ebk.)
Subjects: LCSH: Ertz, Zach, 1990—Juvenile literature. | Football
   players—United States—Biography—Juvenile literature. | Football
   players—Religious life—United States—Juvenile literature.
Classification: LCC GV939.E7 (ebook) | LCC GV939.E7 A3 2019 (print) | DDC
   796.332092 [B] —dc23
LC record available at https://lccn.loc.gov/2019017563

All rights reserved. No part of this publication may be reproduced, stored in a retrieval system, or transmitted in any form or by any means—electronic, mechanical, digital, photocopy, recording, or any other—except for brief quotations in printed reviews, without the prior permission of the publisher.

Printed in the United States of America

19 20 21 22 23 24 25 26 27 / Bang-SK / 10 9 8 7 6 5 4 3 2 1

For Julie.
We love because
He first loved us.

CONTENTS

LET'S GO

FOREWORD BY CARSON WENTZ

If you've heard any of Zach's mic'd up segments during Eagles football games over the last couple of years, you'll notice that one of his favorite phrases is "Let's go!"

"Let's go" can be used in the following contexts:

- when you're about to do something awesome
- when you've just done something awesome
- when somebody else has just done something awesome
- when somebody else needs encouragement
- when you're in one of those "football moments" when people are jumping around and screaming incomprehensible things

"Let's go" is a surprisingly versatile phrase, and I often find myself using it. When I asked Zach to go to Haiti with me a couple of years ago, on a mission trip, his response was, naturally, "Let's go." I think it's safe to say the trip changed Zach's life and took our friendship to another level. And the Lord used it to help Zach and Julie start their family's charitable foundation.

One of the things you need to know about Zach is that he is one of the most "all-in" people I've ever met. When Zach is bought in to something, he buys in completely—whether it's playing soccer with kids on a beat-up field in Haiti, running routes for me after practice, or diving into Scripture to grow in his faith.

I'm so blessed to be teammates and brothers in Christ with Zach. His "Let's go" mentality is infectious. It's also a blessing—one that seems counterintuitive in a football context—that someone who is so dominant and accomplished on the field can be so vulnerable and real off the field. You wouldn't think it by watching us play, but vulnerability is the key to the success we've had on the Eagles and the key to our growth in Christ. And it was in 2016, when Zach was the most vulnerable, that he was able to really taste and see God's goodness for the first time. In a way, it was the beginning of the rest of his life.

And I'm grateful for the way Zach walked with me through some of my most vulnerable moments as a football player, as I rehabbed through injuries and stayed closely connected with my teammates through it all.

One of Zach's other favorite phrases is "Focus and finish," and it applies not only to our football lives but to our spiritual lives. It informs the way Zach reads and discusses the book of Romans, which we did as a team last year. Zach wants to finish well as a player, as a husband, and as a leader of his family. It's how he lives his life, and it's an inspiration to me in my own life and marriage.

I hope you enjoy the stories Zach recounts in these pages, as I've enjoyed experiencing many of them with him. As you read, know that he's sharing these stories from a place of humility. It's not easy for him to talk about himself, so I know this book was written from a loving perspective with the hope that it will encourage those who read it.

Let's go!

Carson Wentz
Quarterback, Philadelphia Eagles

1

THANK YOU, NFL

I n Week 1 of the 2016 season, I hurt my shoulder.

It was a perfect day for football in Philly—75 degrees and sunny—and the crowd was raucous. It was the first pro start for our rookie first-round draft pick Carson Wentz, a quarterback from North Dakota State, and our first game with a brand-new head coach in Doug Pederson. Hopes were high. There was a 9/11 tribute before the game, and soldiers rolled out a giant American flag on the field.

As was the case before every game early in my career, I felt such excitement and anxiety that I was almost physically ill. Life in the NFL is fun, but it's also the most stressful, pressure-filled thing I've ever done. Carson and I walked out onto the field together. My gloves were right, my armbands were right, and the green number 86 jersey felt perfect. We were just getting to know each other then, but now he's one of my best friends.

Our coaches called a great first series to get everyone comfortable playing again. We started with a couple of runs to get Carson acclimated. On our first play, running back Ryan Matthews ran for six yards right behind me. My job was to step inside and collide with Cleveland's defensive end. I was supposed to shoot my play-side hand into his armpit and get my hat in front of his. On the snap, I stepped, and bang! There was a tiny explosion in my helmet, meaning I'd done my job. The first play of 2016 was in the books, and it was a good one.

> It takes a village to raise an NFL player.

Playing tight end in the NFL means that on some plays, I'm blocking guys who are much bigger than me, and on other plays, I might be running a pass pattern or lining up wide in the formation. Later in the series, Carson saw a matchup we both liked. I was lined up wide against a smaller Cleveland safety. Carson threw a fade to my outside shoulder, and I had to swing my body around and adjust to grab it. I snatched the ball out of the air with one hand and crashed to the ground. A catch. My first of the season.

Plays like that allow me to use some of my old basketball skills. Going up against someone to catch a ball is a lot like boxing a guy out down low for a rebound. I use my big body and then let my instincts take over. When I was in middle school and high school, I dreamed about playing in the NBA. I was going to be the next Adam Morrison (more on that later)—until I met a former NFL tight end named Brent Jones, who won some Super Bowls as a member of the San Francisco 49ers. Brent told me that if I worked hard, I could play on Sundays in the NFL. I wouldn't be in the league without him, and my mom, and about 100 other people. It takes a village to raise an NFL player—but more on that later as well. I'm getting ahead of myself!

Something you should know about Carson Wentz is that he never played like a rookie. Even on that first drive, he was cool in the huddle and calmly changed plays at the line of scrimmage. It was like playing in front of 70,000 people on national television didn't even faze him despite never performing on that kind of stage. One of Carson's heroes is Brett Favre, who was a really similar player—a big, athletic dude with a huge arm and no fear, who smiled a lot and had fun playing the game.

EVERYTHING CHANGES

Later in the drive, something happened, and everything changed. We ran one of my favorite plays: I go in motion across the formation, and the receiver to my side runs a slant. I'm supposed to leak out into the flat underneath him, where I'll be wide open with space to run after the catch.

The play worked just like Doug and the staff drew it up. I started moving forward into my route just before the snap, and before I knew it, Carson put the ball right into my hands. I turned upfield and ran for about 13 yards before I slammed into Cleveland's safety Ibraheim Campbell, whose job was to fly up, crash into my left shoulder, and drive me out of bounds.

He did his job perfectly. As soon as I got up, I knew something wasn't right with my shoulder, but there was no time to deal with it. We went right back to the huddle and then into our next play. I had to get down into my stance and block Cleveland's outside linebacker Joe Schobert—at the time, a rookie out of

> "Something doesn't feel right in my shoulder."

Wisconsin playing in his first NFL game. I managed to get my hands on Schobert and move my body in front of him, but my shoulder was on fire.

That first series was perfect for Carson. He hit our receiver Jordan Matthews on a fade route in the end zone, but before I could get my shoulder checked out, I had to stand in as the left-side wing in the field goal unit. My job was to stick my foot in the ground and get a punch on their outside rusher. The extra point is one of those plays that most NFL fans ignore, but in order to get it right, everybody on the field has to do their job. Thankfully, I was able to get a hand on the rusher, and we made the kick.

After the field goal, I jogged over to the sideline and found the trainers. "Something doesn't feel right in my shoulder," I said, and they started lifting my pads and feeling around my arm. In the NFL, there's a lot of adrenaline and caffeine pumping through your body during a game, and you don't necessarily feel all the pain of an injury right away. The trainers thought it was a sprain, so I kept playing.

The rest of the game was a blur. At that time in my life, before I knew Christ, I was living for the stat sheet. If I caught seven balls and a touchdown or two, it meant I had a good day, and I could feel good about myself. If not, there was a lot of anxiety and fear and paranoia. I was living and dying by these performances.

> I was living and dying by these performances.

WHEN THE ADRENALINE WEARS OFF

After an NFL game, you go back to the locker room, the coach says a few words, and then you shower and meet with the media at your locker. Finally, you get to find your family. That night, I was looking for my girlfriend (now my wife), Julie, who is a professional soccer player, and my mom.

It should have been a celebratory night, since we got our first win with a new quarterback and a new coach—and wins of any kind are hard to come by in the NFL. But as the adrenaline wore off, I could barely move my shoulder. I called the team doctor and asked him to check me out the next morning.

For an introverted West Coast kid, adjusting to Philly was really tough. It was a cold, gray, tough East Coast city, and in my early days in the league,

I was away from my family and my girlfriend for the first time. People envision NFL rookies living an amazing life, floating on a cloud of money and going from city to city and party to party, but it's really like having any other job. You go to the office (in my case, the team facility), put in long hours, try to take care of your body, and try to figure out whom to trust.

Obviously, I play a sport that is very taxing on the body. I usually play on Sundays, but I don't feel the real effects until later on. An ankle sprain feels way worse the next morning. Having to get on a flight to get to the next stadium is painful—everything swells up because of the altitude. After my games, I take an inventory of my body. I start with my ankles: "Are you guys good?" Then I ask, "Knees, how are you guys feeling?" I move on to my groin, hips, hamstrings, shoulders, and neck. If something's not right, I have to figure out how I'm going to fix it before taking the field in a few days.

> If something's not right, I have to figure out how I'm going to fix it before taking the field in a few days.

FINDING A ROUTINE

I stick to the same routine every week.

Monday means a two-hour massage. I get acupuncture, where they stick little needless just under my skin. After that, I lift weights and then take an Epsom salt bath.

Tuesday is a complete "off day"—at least physically. I go to the facility with the rest of my teammates for five hours to review the previous game's film and go over a light install for the upcoming week. In the training room, I get my hips worked on and sometimes run on our underwater treadmill.

On Wednesdays, the team has a tough practice where we work on installs for the coming week. Afterward, I stretch and go right into the cold tub, then work with the trainers to make sure my hips are moving well.

Thursday I might get "scraped," which is a Chinese technique that involves scraping muscle tissue to stimulate blood flow. The practice has been used for centuries to promote healing.

> "Zach, you need a routine of greatness."

Friday is a short day at the facility. After that, I go to yoga to decompress mentally and physically. I have another massage, and then I meet up with Julie either at home or someplace in the city for a date night. Needless to say, this is my favorite part of the week!

Saturday means another massage to make sure everything is moving right.

Keeping up with my health and training is truly a weeklong process. Early in my career, I spoke with former NFL tight end (and future Hall of Famer) Tony Gonzalez. Tony played in 14 Pro Bowls and had more than 15,000 career receiving yards. He said, "Zach, you need a routine of greatness. Our routines are not all gonna be the same, but find out what works for you and commit to it. You're not gonna last in this league without a routine."

FEELING USELESS

At the start of my career in Philly, I didn't open up to a lot of people. In football culture, if you're walking down the hall and somebody asks how you're doing, you feel like you have to say "Great!" even if your arm is hanging off and blood is shooting out of an artery. Every conversation is a referendum on your toughness and manhood. It's not like I was going to go up to an NFL legend like Michael Vick and tell him my deepest, darkest fears—I mean, he would have been cool about it, but it's not like we were on that level. Honestly, I was afraid to try to be!

After the Cleveland game in 2016, the team doctors discovered I had a displaced rib that was pressing on a nerve in my shoulder. They said if the rib moved any farther, it could sever the nerve, and I would lose the use of my arm for the rest of my life. I also had a separated shoulder and a torn pectoral muscle. Kind of a big deal.

That injury diagnosis set off one of the toughest years of my life emotionally. Every day I would drive into the facility, park my car, and head to treatment while the rest of the guys went to team meetings, positional meetings, and film review. Even lifting was hard (if not impossible) with my injury, so I felt like the body I had built for football was starting to shrink. Meanwhile, it looked like everyone else was only getting stronger.

While I was injured, people still treated me like a friend and talked to me, but it was different. The year before was my breakout season—I had pulled in more than 70 balls—but in the NFL, it's not "What did you do last year?" but rather "What are you going to do this week?"

Because of my performance the previous year, I had just signed a contract extension. There were high expectations for me now, and I was paranoid. When you're injured in the NFL, you feel useless, and you think, "Are they gonna release me? Am I ever gonna feel right again?"

TREY OF LIGHT

One of the guys I started getting close to on the team was a tight end named Trey Burton, an undrafted rookie free agent out of Florida. Trey is freakishly athletic and fast, as the world would discover a few years later in our Super Bowl win. He can do anything on a football field. But something I noticed about Trey was that the normal ups and downs

> That injury diagnosis set off one of the toughest years of my life emotionally.

every NFL player goes through didn't seem to faze him.

Life in the NFL was tough for Trey initially. He played on the scout team, which means that during practice, he would run the opposing team's plays. He was also expected to be a stud on special teams and ready for his number to be called on offense. It's the lowest rung on the NFL ladder, but he didn't let his situation get to him.

When you're on a football team—traveling together, eating together, and going to meetings together—you really get to know each other. I knew Trey had a peace and a joy about him that I desperately needed. I was envious of it.

I started to confide in him on the sidelines. I even started calling him "my therapist" because he always had a wise word to help me get my head right.

Ironically, when I hurt my shoulder, it was Trey who replaced me in the lineup. We still had a legendary Philadelphia tight end in Brent Celek, and with Trey in the lineup, we were in good hands. He was ready for his opportunity and deserved it.

I returned to the game after a few weeks, but by then, the Eagles were mired in a losing streak. Even though I was better, I was protecting my shoulder and not playing as freely as I used to. On top of that, there was a lot of pressure to win. Philly is the greatest place in the world to play on a successful team, but it's a tough hang when you're not doing well. And even though most NFL players have thick skin, reading negative things in the media and feeling the backlash from fans still really hurts.

> "Are they gonna release me? Am I ever gonna feel right again?"

> Trey had a peace and a joy about him that I desperately needed. I was envious of it.

A BURFICT STORM

I felt lost and anxious and desolate that season, even though statistically I was doing well and would finish the season with more catches on fewer targets than the year before. It all came to a head in Week 13, when we traveled to Cincinnati to play the Bengals. We pride ourselves on being a physical team—all NFL teams do—but the Bengals were *extra* physical. We knew they played through the whistle, and they were led defensively by a guy named Vontaze Burfict, who is a six-foot-two, 255-pound wrecking ball. I played against him in college, and I knew he'd try to get in my head. It's part of his game.

> Every guy I'm supposed to block is a tough guy.

Let me be clear: I don't mind trash talk, and I don't mind playing against physical guys. In the league, there are new challenges every week, and every guy I'm supposed to block is a tough guy. But the situation with Burfict would come to define that season and, in fact, my life.

The play happened in the first quarter. In our game plan, Doug had me all over the formation, but I usually started either in the slot or lined up wide. In the back of my mind that whole season, I was thinking, "If I get hit the wrong way, I could lose the use of my arm forever."

On a third and eight, I was in the slot, and the play had me out on a pass route. Carson took some pressure and ended up scrambling toward the sideline, where he eventually ran out of bounds without taking a hit. The problem was that Burfict was in pursuit, and I had a chance to put a block on him. If I had, Carson would have run out of bounds anyway—but I didn't touch Burfict, and fans and the media lost their minds. If we had won the game, the play would have been forgotten. Unfortunately, we lost 32–14, and my life would never be the same.

Media pundits said I made a half-hearted attempt and that I was a "toreador" with Burfict. (Toreadors are those guys in Spain who get out of the way of bulls.) They were telling Doug to bench me and calling me soft. And it destroyed me. For the first time in my life, my identity as a tough guy—a football player—was called into question. I felt like I was done with football. I didn't think I could ever repair my reputation, and I wasn't sure I even wanted to try.

RELINQUISHING CONTROL

Growing up, my identity was based on football. I felt like if I worked hard enough or gave something up, football would reward me. It became my theology. Not going out on Friday or Saturday nights in college meant I should get more in return because I had invested in the sport. I was living and dying with every practice rep and every stat sheet at the end of every game.

> For the first time in my life, my identity as a tough guy—a football player—was called into question.

I still felt that way in my early days in the NFL. I was lying in bed replaying the Bengals game over and over in my head. I had no peace—none.

Before then, football was something I felt I controlled. In the aftermath, I just surrendered everything. I said, "Jesus, I'm done . . . I submit everything to You." So as it turns out, that play was the best thing that ever happened to me.

The Burfict play happened when Julie and I were engaged, and I got baptized the day before my wedding. Since then, we've grown a lot together in our walk. We are very blessed to have each other because we understand the physical demands and the stress that come with being an athlete. Being married to Julie means having someone who will (a) be in my corner and (b) show me a different viewpoint. It meant so much to have her there through the whole Burfict ordeal.

"It's going to pass," she told me. "It doesn't define who you are as an athlete or as a person." Eventually, I believed her.

2

FINGER
GOGGLES

I was 14 when my parents got divorced.

As the oldest of four brothers, I had a sense about what was going on, but my siblings were in the dark. My parents' marriage just sort of died. It wasn't like in *The Godfather*, where Talia Shire's character is screaming and throwing plates at Carlo. In fact, that would have been more definitive. In our case, it was a quiet, creeping coldness, with our dad spending less and less time at the house and eventually disappearing completely.

What used to be a partnership—with lots of conversation and laughter—was now a solo gig for my mom. But in an affluent, suburban, NorCal way, our divorces, just like our houses, are clean, efficient, and impressive.

> Packing the duffel bag for the overnight stay at my dad's was always the saddest moment.

At the beginning, I would switch between my parents' houses. For some reason, packing the duffel bag for the overnight stay at my dad's was always the saddest moment. While I was cramming underwear, my toothbrush, and workout gear into the bag, I was reminded of everything that was broken.

"CONTROL WHAT YOU CAN CONTROL"

As an introverted guy with no real church life at the time, I didn't know how to deal with what was happening, so I retreated further and further inward. I didn't have anyone to talk to, so I talked to the weights. In football, we have this saying: "Control what you can control." I could control the frequency and intensity of my workouts, so that's what I did. Harder and heavier, day after day. I made my legs and my arms and my shoulders hurt so I wouldn't have to deal with the pain in my heart and in my household. I had always expected my parents to be together, and suddenly they weren't.

> I didn't know then what I know now: Christ can redeem our sinful pasts and make all things new.

I tried not to think about my family as I ran routes. Route running is quiet and solitary, usually done on empty practice fields. It can be therapeutic: Stick your hand in the dirt. Run a 5-yard out. *Thunk*—the satisfying sound of the ball hitting your glove. Jog back. Go on a 12-yard dig. Count your steps, throttle down, break, and *thunk*. Repeat.

In a Christless environment, a failed marriage is just that—an unredeemable failure. You think of it in terms of a large chunk of time wasted. A bad investment in a person who you thought was going to be your partner for life but who, as it turns out, was the wrong call. I didn't know then what I know now: Christ can redeem our sinful pasts and make all things new. Christ can enable the kind of grace that gives any marriage a shot at working. I thank God each day that He is the foundation of my marriage to Julie.

SCHOOL AND SPORTS

I was born in Southern California, Orange County. When I was about seven, my family moved to Northern California. I have three brothers, and we were all involved in sports. We played soccer and baseball and swam competitively, and I loved basketball. In fact, I thought basketball was "my" sport. I loved Kobe Bryant, who was at the height of his career at the time, and Adam Morrison from Gonzaga. Morrison had goofy, floppy hair and a pubescent and awkward mustache, which I emulated. This resulted in some of the most regrettable middle school pictures of all time. (Maybe my agent can scrub them from the internet forever?)

I should add that Morrison totally pulled the mustache off, and if you were a white swingman who could shoot in the northwest in the early 2000s, you wanted to be him. There weren't a lot of cool white dudes in basketball at that time.

That's pretty much what our lives centered on—education and sports. School was always the focus, and sports were secondary. During that time, my mom became and has remained a huge advocate for football. She said,

> I've watched one of my sons [get] taken off the field in an ambulance. I still feel strongly that with the advent of better rules, knowledge of the game, better equipment—football is a very important part of our culture. We need kids outside between 3:00 and 6:00 in the afternoon each day because this is a magical time when young men get themselves into a lot of trouble. I made it clear that there would be no going to the park and smoking pot. Find something to do.

> I'm a pretty girly girl—God gave me four boys. What am I gonna do? The only thing that kept me from going sideways during the divorce was the support of the coaches, team, team parents . . . [and the] ability to sit in the stands. When Zach went to Stanford,

my son would bring all of his friends. In the Kensington borough of Philly and other neighborhoods like it, there is no golf, no tennis. Football is going to save these kids' lives. It's part of my life's work to advocate for football.

NOT A GREAT START

My first experience with youth football was absolutely awful—I hated it. Here's the scene: Your parents drop you off in some parking lot next to a football field and a cleat house in town. A cleat house is a pole barn where they keep helmets, pads, and blocking dummies when they aren't being used on the field. It's basically a huge metal container. All cleat houses everywhere on the planet smell exactly the same—a mixture of grass, sweat, and testosterone.

> They forgot they were addressing a metal container full of children.

You're shuffling around with a bunch of other grade school boys who are just as insecure as you are, but they're all trying to convince each other (and themselves) they're confident. Some guys have phones and iPads to stare at while the rest stand there and try not to look terrified.

You move from station to station getting a bunch of gear that feels weird. The shoulder pads are heavy, and putting a helmet on for the first time feels like trapping your head in a cave. There are older guys from town walking around in windbreakers and dad hats and talking in voices that are a few octaves lower than normal, referring to you as "men." As in "Men, we're gonna have you stand over here in a single-file line while we take care of some paperwork" and "Men, what you have here today is a golden opportunity."

It seemed like they forgot they were addressing a metal container full of children. Little did I know that in a few years, I'd be having the same experience in a much nicer cleat house (Lucas Oil Stadium) with men in NFL windbreakers and NFL dad hats saying the exact same things. Crazy.

Later that night, these guys will gather at a local bar to eat fried mozzarella sticks, drink beer, and "draft" all the children they've just met. I can guarantee that a grand total of zero men in windbreakers saw me in my Adam Morrison phase and thought, "There's a future Pro Bowl tight end." You realize these guys are going to be living out their repressed coaching fantasies through you, and the thought is terrifying.

THE LOW POINT

After the equipment is handed out, you come to the low point in the cleat-house scenario: you're asked to take your shoes off and step onto an industrial-grade scale. The weight limit for youth football at 13 years old is 125 pounds, and you weigh 138. Seconds later, you're having a deep conversation with a florid, sweaty, middle-aged guy named Bob, who's suggesting ways to lose 13 pounds before "training camp." In my experience, Bob suggested cutting out donuts and any of the cereals that tasted good. I did exactly what he recommended—which, as you can imagine, was hard for a middle school kid!

I made weight, but I was still the biggest kid on the team, so they stuck me at left tackle and defensive line. That experience turned out to be an exercise in staring at the grass through my facemask and leaning up against other big kids while the smaller players got to do fun things like catch the ball and run with it (which, as it turns out, is *really* fun). I was stuck on the line through the year and said, "I'm not playing again."

Like most kids, I loved playing EA Sports's *NCAA Football* and other video games with my friends. We would create ourselves as athletes in the game and dream about playing in the big stadiums we saw on television.

When we weren't gaming, we were shooting baskets in somebody's driveway. Despite the divorce, it was a pretty normal childhood.

BETTER THE SECOND TIME AROUND

My mom, who desperately wanted to keep me busy, made me go out for the football team in high school. She wanted my brothers and me to be active and doing something constructive during that three-hour block between school and dinner. Hanging around a park smoking weed and getting into trouble was not an option for us.

> My mom, who desperately wanted to keep me busy, made me go out for the football team in high school so that I could have some friends at my new school.

It was the cleat-house scenario all over again, but this time I had gained some athleticism, and the experience was much different. The high school coaches put me at quarterback and wide receiver on offense and safety on defense. I was six-foot-four and 180 pounds as a freshman, and the Adam Morrison hair was still there—but it would soon be gone.

Monte Vista High School in Danville was the kind of California school you see in Hollywood movies. We walked outdoors to get to our classes and had a sprawling, sun-drenched campus with a red-tiled roof.

I had the most fun playing football in high school, and I loved spending that time with my friends. There was no real stress about winning or about how I was performing. I put on 20 pounds of muscle each year, so by the time I was a senior, I weighed in at 230 or 240. I loved Friday nights under the lights in our all-red uniforms. Checking out my number 5 jersey and Riddell Revo helmet in the mirror one last time. Leaving the locker room together. Hearing the cleats clacking on the concrete. Hearing our school band play for us.

My mom says she watches my games through "finger goggles"—meaning she puts her hands over her face and peeks out through her fingers to make sure I get up after every play. I don't blame her; it's a violent game. She started doing that in high school and still does it every time I suit up for the Eagles.

THE RIGHT GUY AT THE RIGHT TIME

But I still loved basketball. I was the MVP on the junior varsity team as a freshman. My sophomore year, I played varsity basketball and varsity football. I felt like I was more successful at basketball—I still thought it was my sport. Going into my junior year, my football coach reached out to a guy named Brent Jones.

I didn't know it at the time, but Jones was an NFL legend. He played college football at Santa Clara and then had a long career with the San Francisco 49ers. He appeared in four Pro Bowls and won three Super Bowl titles. Coach Jones got to catch passes from Joe Montana and Steve Young, two of the greatest quarterbacks of all time, and if you watch those Super Bowl highlight shows on ESPN, he's in a bunch of them. It was pretty cool—and a huge, "random" opportunity that fell right into my lap. Looking back, I believe God put this man in my life.

Coach Jones was my first real mentor. You might think a guy with his résumé would ride around in limousines and wear expensive sunglasses all the time, but he was extremely laid-back and made practicing fun. "Now let's go catch some passes!" he would say after we had hit the blocking sled for a while.

> I had the most fun playing football in high school, and I loved spending that time with my friends.

He taught me how to understand and approach route running when I was just 16 years old. Because of him, I could recognize zone versus man coverage and alter my routes accordingly. It was master's-level stuff for a kid my age.

> I was amazed that somebody believed in me.

The most important thing he did, though, was to instill a level of confidence in me. "If you dedicate yourself to the game and to the craft, you can play in the NFL," he said. Needless to say, he knew what he was talking about—and he was right—but at that age, I was just flattered and astounded by the whole thing. I was amazed that somebody believed in me on that level.

RECRUITING LETTERS

Mom sacrificed a lot for my brothers and me. She put all her effort and energy into her kids and made sure nothing slipped. She didn't have a personal life, and she didn't go out and do what most single people in her position would do. I'm obviously very grateful and will never be able to repay her for that kind of sacrifice. My siblings and I were always picked up and dropped off on time, and there was always a meal on the table for us.

> It was cool walking to the mailbox every day—or sometimes getting called out of class—to get a letter from a different college.

As a 16-year-old kid, I was focused on being the best high school player I could be. I went off the first game of my junior year and started getting recruiting letters from places like Northwestern and Arizona. I was also getting letters from Ivy League schools that wanted me for their basketball programs. When you're a kid with a certain height and weight profile in an affluent NorCal high school that serves as a talent pipeline to so many schools, you're kind of on people's recruiting radar by default.

It was cool walking to the mailbox every day—or sometimes getting called out of class—to get a letter from a different college. Each letter represented a different dream. I would think about living in a different city or pulling on a different uniform on a Saturday afternoon. In a way, the letters also represented the culmination of a lot of hard work and served as validation that I could actually play at the next level if I wanted to.

My mom made the decision easy for me when she said, "You're going to Stanford."

Things were going well until I fractured my wrist early in that junior season. After that, I didn't really know what to expect in terms of recruitment. But Coach Jones had a connection with Head Coach Jim Harbaugh at Stanford, and UCLA made a compelling pitch. For a high school kid, the UCLA offer was a hard thing to walk away from—there was the Hollywood aspect, the sunshine, the campus, and the amazing powder-blue jersey with their iconic shoulder stripe.

When it came to visiting schools, I always enjoyed the process. The football staff would take me on a special tour of the facility, show me their uniforms (unlimited shoes, gloves, and swag), and then lead me into a theater, where I would watch highlight film from the season before. I felt proud in those moments because I knew my parents were dreaming big too. As you can imagine, Coach Harbaugh was a persuasive recruiter. He's an impressive-looking guy, and his reputation as a former first-round pick who played in the NFL commands respect.

Stanford offered me a full ride a month after I broke my wrist, and my mom made the decision easy for me when she said, "You're going to

Stanford"—even though I was partial to UCLA. Nobody was thinking about the NFL at that time, and she knew I'd make great connections at Stanford and get a world-class education—both of which were entirely true. When I drove down to Stanford and committed, Coach Harbaugh literally jumped into my arms! Nobody will ever accuse him of lacking enthusiasm.

3

CARDINAL RULES

Practices at Stanford were long and physical. We did Oklahoma drills on the first day of every spring and summer practice. Oklahoma drills can vary, but they essentially amount to this: A blocker, a defensive player or two, and a ball carrier line up between some agility dummies that are laid out a few yards apart on the ground. On the snap of the ball, they slam into each other.

It's a test of their courage and manhood as well as a way to put the techniques they've learned to the test. It's a high-energy moment in a practice, with the whole team gathering around the players to encourage them. Everybody ends up bruised and bloody at the end, but it's a real bonding moment for a team.

Early on, football at Stanford was a grind. I would think about the Oklahoma drill all day leading up to practice. I imagined myself coming off the ball, getting my hands in the right place, and getting the leverage I needed to win the drill. The whole program there was based on competition. It didn't

> The goal was to keep improving day by day.

matter if you were a fifth-year senior or a freshman—it'd be a linebacker against a tight end. Even the receivers and defensive backs would have to go. You'd get a snap count and then *boom!* The moment of impact. Neither side wanted to be embarrassed. Everyone wanted to win. The goal was to keep improving day by day.

Coach Harbaugh was all football all the time. Whenever he pulled a player aside, he wasn't talking about his favorite movies or the player's feelings; it was always the game. The moment he walked into the room, we were on our toes. If you did well on the field, he would be encouraging, but if you weren't doing well, he would remind you. He was exactly what I needed as an 18-year-old.

Coming out of high school, I was the best athlete at my school and the best in the area. I was mentally and physically humbled in my first season at Stanford. I would get dressed in that palatial locker room and realize that every single dude in there was the stud of his high school, his conference, and maybe his state. It was a lot.

You never knew what you were going to get with Coach Harbaugh, and you were always on edge. Even the football building itself was intimidating. There was a hall-of-fame feel to it as you walked in and saw larger-than-life images of Stanford legends like John Elway, Jim Plunkett, and Bill Walsh.

> I was mentally and physically humbled in my first season at Stanford.

There were signs on the walls that said things like "Stanford, not a four-year decision but a lifetime decision." It was hard to think of it that way, as I was just trying to live through each day.

The facility is a constant reminder of all the Stanford players who made it to the NFL. The quarterback room is named for Plunkett and Elway. Even the player's lounge, where guys relax and play pool, is plastered with pictures of Stanford guys who played in the league.

There's so much money invested in the program, it's hard not to be reminded—all the time—of what a huge business college football is. And with a huge business comes a lot of pressure. They had a lot invested in us, literally and figuratively, as a recruiting class. I didn't want to let them down.

> They had a lot invested in us . . . I didn't want to let them down.

FRESHMAN FRIDAYS

It just wasn't that fun in my redshirt year. At times I thought, "I'm just gonna go and play basketball someplace." One of my best friends was on the basketball team at Columbia, and I thought about going to play there. But then I started having little wins in practice—like going against the defense on the scout team and lighting them up.

That year, the coaches held "Freshman Friday" scrimmages for young guys and redshirts. It was a 20-minute scrimmage before all the veteran players came out on the field, and it was a blast. If you did well, you got to travel with the team to away games. It meant a lot to me to be able to travel because it felt like I was contributing to the team even though I was redshirted.

GRINDING

That first year was extremely difficult and contained more lows than highs. I had the worst GPA of my career because I didn't know how to study and manage my time as a college athlete. My first year, I redshirted, which was exactly what I needed at the time. I was in the weight room grinding for two hours every day. I was pushing myself at practice without the promise of the stadium lights at the end of the tunnel on game days. Blocking fully grown defensive ends as an 18-year-old tight end was difficult, but it only made me stronger in the end.

Tight end is one of the tougher positions to play. You're involved in every aspect of the game plan. You have to know the passing game as well as the quarterback, every spot on the offense, and all the intricacies of the run game. Mentally, it's extremely difficult, and physically, you're going to be outmatched in the run game. Most of the guys you block are bigger and stronger than you, so your technique has to be on point—the best it can be.

Our 2009 recruiting class was ranked third in the Pac-12 and twenty-first nationally—impressive for a school where every athlete has to qualify per the admission standards (which isn't the case everywhere). We had studs like Tyler Gaffney, Shayne Skov, and Terrence Stephens, and we were getting to know each other via group texts before we even hit campus. That bond, more than anything, helped me survive that first year.

GETTING STRONGER

Early on, I was drawn to Owen Marecic, who was an upperclassman and a two-way superstar as a fullback and linebacker. Owen was a beast and a throwback. He didn't wear gloves and was a human biology major who wanted to be a doctor. He allegedly did yoga and meditation and was a really unusual dude. To me, he was a brute-force type of guy. He was lightly recruited, relatively speaking, in that his only offers were Army, Yale, and Stanford. But he was a super-effective player and once scored two touchdowns in 13 seconds—one on a running play and the other on a pick-six. He was remarkable.

> We would call three plays in the huddle, and our quarterback was in charge of getting us into the best one.

It's tough for a non–football player to appreciate how incredibly hard it is to play both offense and defense at any level, peewee or high school, much less in the Pac-12. Owen is a Stanford legend, and rightfully so—that dude was an animal!

Our strength coach would rave about Owen's work ethic. I took note and one day asked, "Hey, man, can I follow you around in the summer?" He was cool about it. We'd do double sessions in the weight room. After the morning workout, we'd come back in the evenings and do it again. It was exactly what I needed to get stronger and stay disciplined. I always wanted to make sure I was there on time and did not keep him waiting.

In terms of growing up and becoming a man, no one served as a better role model than Jim Harbaugh. He was hard on everybody. The physical toughness and the mental toughness were there on our team. On Saturdays, we were ready to go. We had a pro-style system: we would call three plays in the huddle, and our quarterback was in charge of determining the best one. Maintaining that kind of offense was asking a lot of a college player. As a tight end, I had to be able to block for Harbaugh. He took pride in running the ball behind fullbacks and tight ends.

PAYOFF

I saw my first ever action in a college game during my second year, playing against Sacramento State at home. We had some real stars on that offense—guys like Doug Baldwin, Stepfan Taylor, and a quarterback named Andrew Luck, whom you may have heard of.

I caught a touchdown in that game and felt like all my hard work had paid off. It was an unbelievable feeling. Moments like those kept me in the right frame of mind moving forward.

> Andrew Luck... one of the most talented dudes I've ever been around.

Later in that season, we had a chance to play on the road against Cal in the stadium I grew up going to as a kid. I would go to games with my dad, buy a program, go down close to the field to watch the players warm up, and envision myself playing in an environment like that.

Stanford versus Cal, the "Big Game," is one of the most infamous rivalries in college football, especially for West Coast kids. In 1982, the Cal kick-return team kept the play alive by lateraling the ball all the way down the field. They eventually scored and ran over some band kids who had wandered onto the field because they thought the play was over. Everybody gets hyped for the Big Game, and the tension is high.

FINDING LUCK

Did I mention that my college quarterback was Andrew Luck? People forget a few things about Andrew—namely, that he's huge and that he's a really fast, talented runner. He was on fire in the Cal game with his passes, and he had a long run in the first quarter where he trucked one of their guys and barely broke stride. I hustled downfield and got a couple of blocks in, but honestly, Andrew didn't need them. But even then I was trying to counteract the reputation I had for just wanting to be a "receiving tight end."

The Andrew Luck you see in the media is the same guy you see off the field. He's kind of aloof—a goofball, a nice guy, but a freak of an athlete. The strength coaches would have to pull him back from lifting too much because everything they'd throw on the bar would be too light for him. Andrew could jump out of the gym and would dunk on dudes during pickup basketball games. It always shocked people that a white guy with an Amish-style beard was that athletic. In terms of perfecting his craft, nobody worked harder than him. He took difficult classes and got As. He is truly one of the most talented dudes I've ever been around.

I also felt like Andrew and I were kindred spirits in terms of our obsession with football. One day I told him, "If you ever want to throw on the side, lemme know." For a while, I didn't hear anything, but then during finals week, I got a call.

"Hey, Zach," Andrew said. "Let's go throw. Let's go get some work in."

So on a Saturday in the spring, we went out to the practice field at Stanford and worked on our craft. After that, we spent more time together.

Once while we were playing basketball, I dunked on him in a one-on-one game. He just started laughing.

"Wait, did you just dunk on me in one-on-one?" he asked.

Most guys would talk trash or take it personally, but not him. He was very comfortable in his own skin—comfortable and confident and one of the most competitive people I've ever known. If he threw an interception, he'd be hot.

In the off-season, Andrew and I would be pitted against each other in sprints and sled pushes, since quarterbacks and tight ends have similar body types and are both considered "big-skill" guys. There was no "I'll win this one, you win that one"—that's the mentality we had, and it reflected the approach the Stanford program had to every game.

Everybody talks about Andrew's arm strength, but his accuracy was incredible too. In the second quarter of that Cal game, I ran a deep-post route and was blanketed pretty well by the safety who was covering me. But Andrew put the ball right on my numbers in the end zone, where only I could catch it, and I was able to score a touchdown in a rivalry game in a place that was special to me. With each game, I grew more and more confident that I belonged on a college football field.

FUN IN MIAMI

That 2010 team ended up being pretty special. We finished the regular season 11–1, ranked fifth in the country in the AP poll. We would have won the national championship if they had the college football playoff! We beat USC at home and had a big win against Notre Dame on the road in South Bend. I only had 16 catches that season, but I scored five touchdowns.

There were some established tight ends on that roster who would go on to play in the NFL, including Coby Fleener. Andrew was obviously the first pick in the draft a couple years later, and we also had Ryan Whelan, Griff Whalen, Doug Baldwin, Konrad Rueland, Levine Toilolo, Jonathan Martin, David Decastro, Stepfan Taylor, Tyler Gaffney, Chris Owusu, and Owen Marecic—all of whom would also play in the NFL.

> Our version of "going out" was to go to Foot Locker or Champs and see if there was something we wanted to buy.

And that was just the offense. Defensively, we had Richard Sherman, Michael Thomas, Trent Murphy, Shayne Skov, and Owen Marecic (again). There was just so much talent up and down the line.

The season culminated in a trip to the Orange Bowl in Miami against Virginia Tech. I hadn't traveled to the East Coast much, and it was my first time playing in an NFL stadium. Bowl trips are a nice reward for a season of hard work. We spent the week in Miami going to different functions in the evening and practicing during the day.

I was 20 at the time, but our version of "going out" was to go to Foot Locker or Champs and see if there was something we wanted to buy. We stayed in this swanky hotel and spa in Miami Beach called the Fontainebleau, which sits right on the ocean. It was a shock to sit in those luxury rooms in the complimentary robes and realize that I was there because I could catch a football.

> Harbaugh was coming up to me all week, grabbing me by the back of the neck, saying, "Zach, you're doing a great job."

Despite the venue, Harbaugh was all business. It was New Year's Eve that week, and Jamie Foxx and DJ Tiësto were there performing a show right outside the hotel. We could hear the music through the walls, but we were trying to sleep because we had bed checks.

After that New Year's night, everyone's iPhones got messed up. I missed the special-teams meetings the next morning because my alarm didn't go off. I realized I missed the meeting and thought, "Oh my gosh, that is absurd!" Initially, my position coach told me I might be benched, and I was crushed because Harbaugh had been coming up to me all week, grabbing the back of the neck, saying, "Zach, you're doing a great job." Thankfully, my playing time wasn't reduced.

It seemed like drama always followed Coach Harbaugh. In the week leading up to the Orange Bowl, there were rumors that he might take a head coaching job with the Broncos, the 49ers, or even the University of Michigan. But we blocked it out, and then we went out against Virginia Tech and set the world on fire. The other tight end set the record for catches. I ran a skinny post in the second quarter, and as usual, Andrew put the ball right on the money. I was able to gather it in and tumble into the end zone for the touchdown that would put us ahead. We never looked back and went on to win the game 42–12.

2011: GAME READY

We were ranked in the top five teams heading into 2011, so we had high expectations even though Coach Harbaugh had moved on to the NFL and was replaced by David Shaw. We were running three tight-end sets because we had a ton of talent among Fleener, Levine Toilolo, and me. Even though we lost a lot of coaches, we expected a national championship. That year, we ran the three tight-end sets out of no huddle, and no one could stop us. Andrew had a template of the plays he liked, and he would get us in the right plays every time—all from the line of scrimmage. I can't overstate how unique that is for a college quarterback.

I got hurt and missed the first significant amount of playing time of my career in 2011. We played USC at the LA Coliseum, which is a huge, historic stadium. They had a good team that year, with Matt Barkley at quarterback. They had the band, the song girls, the classic uniforms, the Trojan on the horse, and all the Hollywood glitz and glamour, with celebrities like Will Ferrell and Snoop Dogg on the sidelines. On the opening kickoff, while I was blocking my guy, the tackler missed the kick returner and dove right into my leg. I heard a pop, but I refused to lie on the ground. I had heard stories of a former Stanford Cardinal tight end, Jim Dray, who suffered a knee injury and crawled off the field. I didn't want that to be me. I got up but could barely put any weight on my leg. I got about ten yards from our sideline when the

> The other two tight ends carried me off the field.

other two tight ends saw me and knew
something was wrong. They came over,
I put one arm around each of them, and
they carried me off the field.

"Adversity doesn't build
character; it reveals it."

I had a grade-three medial collateral
ligament (MCL) sprain, and if you watch the film, you can see Andrew coming onto the field, looking at me lying there on the grass.

OUT OF SIGHT, OUT OF MIND

It was my first time experiencing an injury of that magnitude, and it made me realize that on a football team, when you're out of sight, you're out of mind. The coaches immediately turn their attention to the next guy. Someone else is getting your reps in practice and catching the balls that normally go to you in games. The season goes on.

I was living in the training room. I'd get there at 7:00 a.m. and read a book called *Lone Survivor* that our strength coach had given me. Inside was an inscription that said, "Adversity doesn't build character; it reveals it." That really resonated with me at the time, and I said, "I'm gonna do everything I can to not regret anything about this." I was on and off the "Game Ready," which is a state-of-the-art machine that pumps heat or cold or stimulation into a wrap that goes around the injured body part. There was a big NASA station by Stanford, and I even went there a few times to get therapy, figuring that if it was good enough for the space program, it was good enough for me.

STUDENT FIRST, ATHLETE SECOND

It was very tough to get to class at the time, since Stanford has such a big campus. The athletic department gave me a golf cart to get around. At

Stanford, student athletes are expected to do well in school. I was in class with the guy who started Snapchat and a bunch of other future business leaders. My status as a football player didn't earn me any stares or special treatment. I was there for the same reason as everyone else—to go to school.

I had a chip on my shoulder when it came to academics because when I said I was going to Stanford, a lot of people from my high school were like, "Yeah, right." They didn't think I could cut it. So I decided I was going to do everything I could to make the All Pac-12 Academic team and become an All-American. I didn't do much outside of football and class. I didn't really drink back then (and still don't), but when guys would go out drinking, I would just hang.

> I had a chip on my shoulder when it came to academics because when I said I was going to Stanford, a lot of people from my high school were like, "Yeah, right." They didn't think I could cut it.

My philosophy was that we had just spent three hours in the weight room doing everything we could to improve as football players, and even if there was a small chance of my training being ruined by going out, it wasn't a risk I was going to take. I kept thinking about the mantra that was printed on a huge banner at the practice field: "You are either getting better or you are getting worse; you never stay the same." That always resonated with me. We had a few other guys who were like me, which made it easier to abstain from alcohol and partying.

A PACKED SCHEDULE

Even back then, my goal was to leave college early so I could go to the pros. Setting goals was and still is huge for me. Being an athlete meant I never had a lot of time. I had to stack classes back-to-back, and most of my teammates were in the same situation. One was running back Toby Gerhart. He was a monster. Toby wore number 7 and rushed for more than 1,800 yards in 2009 on his way to winning the Doak Walker Award and the Jim Brown Trophy.

When I was redshirted, I got to watch Toby every Saturday in person. Each game, he put on a show, and the Jacksonville Jaguars made him their second-round pick.

I was in stretch lines one day with another freshman, and we were talking about what major we should declare. Stretch lines are when we all line up in a grid after practice and get our bodies stretched out. It's one of the few periods during practice when we're allowed to banter a little bit and don't have to be laser focused.

Toby overheard us and said, "Hey, if you can major in management science and engineering, you guys should do it."

We looked at each other, thinking, "If it's good enough for Toby, it's good enough for us," because this guy was like a god to us. So from that moment on, I told myself, "I'm gonna major in management science and engineering."

Because of the constraints on my time, my teammates were my biggest influence at Stanford. As much as I would have loved to get coffees and have deep discussions with professors outside of class, that wasn't going to happen with how packed my schedule was as a student and a football player.

But in 2011, my focus was on getting back from the sprained MCL as soon as possible. I got back in three and a half weeks and had to play in a *huge* brace. My feeling was, "I *need* to play. I'm *gonna* play," because, remember, football was

> Football was my idol at the time, and it was my only way of securing little pellets of affirmation.

my idol at the time, and it was my only way of securing little pellets of affirmation from the universe. I wasn't even remotely ready to answer the "Who is Zach Ertz without football?" question, which was always at the back of my mind. The only way I could stave off answering it was through more hard work and more success. But I knew that at a place like Stanford, there were young guys behind me who were the studs of *their* high school conferences, and they were all too happy to take my spot. Football is an "eat or be eaten" kind of ecosystem.

> Football is an "eat or be eaten" kind of ecosystem.

FIESTA BOWL BOUND

I declared myself healthy and came back for our game against Notre Dame. The Notre Dame game is a nonconference matchup, but that team always felt like a rival. There is also a big trophy for whoever wins called the jeweled shillelagh (a sort of Irish walking stick–type weapon). Like us, they're a private, academically elite school with a ton of tradition. I had only one catch for zero yards, but it didn't matter because we won the game and found out we were going to the Fiesta Bowl.

Before the bowl game, I graduated to a smaller knee brace. We were playing Oklahoma State University (OSU) at University of Phoenix Stadium (now State Farm Stadium), where the Arizona Cardinals play. As bowl sites go, Tempe was a little bit lower key than Miami—at least, there were no big rap concerts happening outside our hotel windows.

Our opening drive foreshadowed some unfortunate things to come. We moved easily down the field—largely on the back of a long Stepfan Taylor run—but then failed to convert a field goal. Still, my knee felt warm, and I felt good.

Their quarterback, Brandon Weeden, who had played several years of pro baseball, threw a pick on his first attempt, and we were back in business. Shortly after the turnover, our receiver Ty Montgomery (who is now an NFL running back) caught a drag across the middle and got absolutely blown up by one of their guys. The hit was so violent, Ty's helmet flew off—it was the kind of tackle that would come with an ejection today in college football. Ty would get his revenge on our next drive, though, catching a long skinny post for a touchdown.

We racked up 590 yards of total offense, including 347 passing yards and two touchdown passes from Andrew Luck (one of which went to me) and 177 rushing yards and two touchdowns from Stepfan Taylor. We just couldn't put them away, and OSU kept things close, forcing four ties but never taking the lead until the game's final play. OSU quarterback Brandon Weeden and receiver Justin Blackmon connected for three touchdown passes, but ultimately, the game was decided by special teams.

WINNING AND LOSING TOGETHER

The score was tied 38–38 in the fourth quarter, and we had a chance to win it in regulation. We ran the ball a few times, and then Jordan Williamson, our kicker, hooked a 35-yarder to the left. He missed a 43-yarder in overtime—again left—but it wasn't all his fault, as the snap was a little low. The fact of the matter is that teams win and lose *together*, and no loss is ever on the shoulders of one guy.

Still, we had no business losing the game, and it was gut-wrenching. Our locker room was silent. Guys ripped off their tape jobs and walked to the shower

> I was proud of our team because no one pointed the finger in the locker room.

in silence. Everybody was bruised and beaten, and our uniforms were stained from the stadium turf. It was my first experience of failure on a big stage like that, and it hurt. There are no words that can take away that kind of pain. We had been so good for so long, but I was proud of my team because no one pointed the finger in the locker room. In fact, our All-American guard David DeCastro got in a shouting match with some media people because they kept surrounding Williamson's locker.

Andrew Luck had a big influence on me and my confidence at that time. When I was in spring ball after my freshman year, a lot of NFL scouts came to practice. I was like, "Man, that's cool that those guys are looking at Coby Fleener."

Andrew said, "Zach, they're gonna be looking at you and Levine in not too long."

He was right, but I didn't know it at the time. And before I started seriously thinking about the NFL, the Lord changed my life in a huge way.

4

JULIE

When I started my junior year at Stanford, I had no idea that my life was about to change forever—for the better—and that change had absolutely nothing to do with football.

One spring afternoon, I went to the stadium at Stanford after a workout to watch a high school friend of mine pitch a game. He was an absolute monster on the mound and ended up being the number-one pick of the MLB draft. That's when I first saw Julie Johnston, a sophomore at Santa Clara.

I really went inward when my parents got divorced.

I knew right away that she didn't go to Stanford because I never would have forgotten her if I had seen her around campus. There was an open seat next to her, and I did a very uncharacteristic thing: I went up and sat right next to her. This was crazily out of character for me, as I was always kind of shy with girls. My friends couldn't believe it, but I guess it was just the way it was supposed to be.

I was still an introvert at heart and said more about the sunflower seeds we were sharing than any other topic. Still, I found it extremely easy to talk to her, which was unique because I really went inward when my parents got divorced. I didn't open up to anyone and normally just kept to myself. I didn't bring up the fact that I was a football player, and she didn't bring up the fact that she was a soccer player. We talked about our lives outside of sports, and I loved that. College baseball games are great settings for conversation, and that afternoon was perfect—warm and quiet—and I could really get to know her.

> She was able to pull me—my *entire* personality—out of my shell.

A few months went by, and we kept in touch through Facebook. We hung out in November of my last season at Stanford, and from then on, we were inseparable. She was able to pull me—my *entire* personality—out of my shell. I was able to be myself around her. I started being more and more open with her and fell further and further in love with her.

We didn't know what we wanted to do or what the future was going to hold. She didn't know if she could date a pro athlete who might end up in some faraway location (as I eventually would), but I was determined to make it work. One night I said, "We're gonna do this thing wherever I am. Let's see how this thing turns out."

Julie is super outgoing and likes to joke and have a good time. She is so authentic all the time. We did a lot of long-distance dating at the beginning of our relationship *and still do*!

EMOTIONS: GREAT SERVANTS, HORRIBLE MASTERS

As Julie and I grew closer, my faith continued developing. Our marriage was built on Christ as the foundation. If we weren't rooted in Christ, we would have no chance at this thing with the temptations we face. Having our personal relationship in line, for us, means having our ship with Christ in line. That's at the center of everythi~ lean on when times are tough. I trust her relationship she trusts mine.

As humans, we're going to fall all the time, and that are able to navigate together in Christ. Getting to know j faith in the idea that a relationship could survive if it was bu and peace. I don't understand how people get through rela marriage without Christ. Relationships are so challenging, I ca ...agine what my marriage would look like without Scripture guiding Julie and me through repentance, reconciliation, and the Gospel. I think a lot of people who are believers would say the same thing.

Julie is a FIFA Women's World Cup champion and plays as a midfielder for the Chicago Red Stars of the National Women's Soccer League, the highest division of women's professional soccer in the country, and the United States women's national soccer team.

> Athletes are sometimes emotional people.

I'm so thankful Julie is an athlete. She understands so many things that the typical nonathlete wouldn't be able to. Having someone who truly appreciates the on- and off-field challenges is *so valuable*.

Julie is my copilot and my voice of reason. When I'm trying to recover from an injury, sometimes I need her to say, "Don't rush back; understand the big picture." Having her means having somebody to restore my confidence when I'm not playing well. She also helps me deal with my coaches and teammates. Athletes are sometimes emotional people. Emotions are great servants but horrible masters. When I explain what I think is going on, she might say, "Take a deep breath. Maybe they're *not* trying to avoid throwing you the ball. Step back and see another perspective."

Understanding each other's training demands is also important. For example, if it's Saturday, sometimes one of us has to train. Julie will say, "I gotta get a run and a lift in," and I totally get it. With normal couples, it's "Let's go for a walk" or "Let's hang out and watch TV." With us, I'll run her through her lift, and then she's on the treadmill for an hour. It means understanding the ebbs and flows, the hills and valleys, of her job.

> The question was always, "Are your habits reflecting the mission you stated?"

I love watching Julie play soccer. I love seeing the joy and the intensity she plays with, and I love seeing her hard work pay off. I do get nervous at times during some of her highly competitive games, when she's playing very physically. As an athlete, you want to feel like you have control of each outcome, but in those situations, I have no control. Most of it is just enjoyment.

I don't think too much about injuries. I don't want to talk about the risks of chronic traumatic encephalopathy (CTE) or anything like that with her. Julie and I understand that those risks are part of the game. We pray that they're not going to happen, but we understand that if there is an injury, it's part of the plan.

SETTING GOALS

Back at Stanford, I was putting everything into my education so I could graduate in four years. I took summer school just to get ahead of my course load. I wanted to take a quarter off so I could train for the combine.

Early on, I didn't really consider the NFL. Then a couple tight ends on my team got drafted, and I remember thinking, "I can play with those guys. I think there's a chance that if I commit myself to this, I might be just as good—or maybe even better." I made it a goal. I started working toward numbers on the field and in the weight room. I told myself I had to do double days in the summer for three years. The NFL was my big goal, but one of my little goals along the way was to win the Mackey Award (given to the best tight end in the nation). The strength coaches at Stanford made the team set individual goals. We wrote them down on pieces of paper and turned them in. The question was always, "Are your habits reflecting the mission you stated?"

> God's timing was perfect for my marriage and when I came to Christ.

It was common to have scouts at Stanford practices, but anytime we saw a guy in the corner with an Eagles or Colts or a Bears shirt on, it was much easier to get ourselves ready that day during training camp! It was fun having them there because they were reminders of our goals and reminders of what was on the line. It elevated our level of play.

I was oblivious to spiritual things while I was at Stanford. I don't remember having too many outspoken Christian teammates there, and if I did, I didn't know who they were. I would go to Mass on Easter and Christmas, but it felt more like just going through the motions. I didn't understand and have the wisdom that I have now. There was so much I didn't know—so much I wish I knew. But God's timing was perfect for my marriage and when I came to Christ.

MY FINAL SEASON AT STANFORD

That last year at Stanford, I knew I'd be a big part of the offense. Coach Shaw was not quite as intense as Jim Harbaugh on the field, but his desire to win is second to none. He just portrays it differently. When Harbaugh went to the 49ers, our first training camp with Shaw was tougher than it was with Harbaugh.

I remember being in the meal room with the guys, saying, "Coach Harbaugh used to give us a night off each training camp to go to the movies" . . . but it never came. That set the stage for his tenure as a coach. Camp was difficult that year. Everything hurt—my legs, my shoulders, my neck, even my teeth—but it was worth it.

> Coach Shaw truly cared about me as a player and my career, not just what was best for his program.

I led the country in catches and yards by a tight end that year, so right after the season was over and while I was doing bowl prep, I sent my papers into the league to get a sense for where I might be drafted. The league has a clearinghouse where you can be vetted by scouts and personnel people if you're considering leaving college early to declare for the draft.

Coach Shaw pulled me aside and said, "Hey, it looks like you're going in the second round."

I thought about going back for my senior season because the first round was always my dream, but he said, "No, you should leave." He knew what was best for me. He had been in the league, and he knew what it took.

I respected him a lot for that. Coach Shaw truly cared about me as a player and my career, not just what was best for his program.

It wasn't easy leaving my teammates. In a weird twist of fate, we played UCLA twice, back-to-back, in the last game of the season and then again six days later in the conference championship, which we came from behind to win 27–24.

> The Rose Bowl is a classic stadium and a classic bowl game. If you're a West Coast kid, it's the one you dream of playing in.

That victory was sweet because I almost went to UCLA and because our kicker Jordan Williamson got a bit of redemption, hitting two key kicks late, including the game winner. That meant we were Pac-12 champs and were headed to the Rose Bowl to play Wisconsin.

THE ROSE BOWL

The Rose Bowl is a classic stadium and a classic bowl game. If you're a West Coast kid, it's the one you dream of playing in. We had a special team in 2012—Kevin Hogan took over for Andrew Luck at quarterback, and Stepfan Taylor and Shayne Skov were both seniors. On paper, it maybe wasn't as loaded as our previous teams, but we played really well together.

There's a lot of pageantry associated with the Rose Bowl. We had our team media days at Disneyland in Anaheim and some events with both teams in Beverly Hills the week before the game. Wisconsin was no stranger to this game, as they'd played in the Rose Bowl the previous two years.

The game itself didn't feature a lot of offense. I led our team in receiving with just three catches and 61 yards, one of which was a 43-yarder, and then I had a key catch in the fourth quarter. But we did a lot of work on the ground and took what Wisconsin gave us. We won 20–14, and Coach Shaw became the first African American head coach to win a Rose Bowl as well as a Bowl Championship Series game.

I remember standing in the locker room after the game with my teammate and fullback Ryan Hewitt. We were both wearing our Nike Stanford Football shirts, with our arms all bruised from the game, being interviewed by a TV guy. Those are the memories—beat up but happy with a win with your teammates—that you never forget. It's part of what's unique about college and part of what made it so hard to leave.

5

NO REGRETS

Making the move to the NFL was a difficult decision. Stanford had won its first Pac-12 Championship as a program, and I thought we could contend for a national title my senior year. I talked with my parents and some agents. They said, "You should probably come out." So after the Rose Bowl, I decided it was time for me to go.

PREPARING FOR THE NFL COMBINE

As soon as I made the decision, I had to start preparing for the NFL Scouting Combine. I trained for the specific events that are held at the combine, including the three-cone 40-yard dash, the vertical jump, the broad jump, and field work. I had no off time to heal my body. I went right from a bowl game in January to prepping for an event that would take place in February.

For me, there was no question as to where I'd do my combine prep. A friend in the Bay Area named Dave Spitz founded a gym when I was in high school and started training guys for the combine. I would go back to his gym, called Cal Strength, and train when I was home on breaks from college. Dave is no longer just a "trainer" to me—he is family. He was even in my wedding party.

I decided early on I would stay at my mom's house and have my agent help her with the rent so I could train at Cal Strength with Dave. I trusted him, which is the most important factor in any relationship, and I understood that he could help me produce the results I needed.

> Dave Spitz is no longer just a trainer to me—he is family. He was even in my wedding party.

As an added bonus, he trained my Stanford teammate Shayne Skov at the same facility, along with Kiko Alonso, who would go on to become an NFL star. Our receiver Chris Owusu had trained there the previous year. In addition to combine prep, Cal Strength provides athletes with tailored nutrition programs, public relations coaching, and general mentorship. The experience was second to none.

FULL CIRCLE

The cool thing about training at Cal Strength was that our on-field work actually took place at Monte Vista High, where I had gone to high school. It felt like I had come full circle, or close to it. We would do weights in the mornings and core lifts like squats and cleans and bench, which were all meant to get us ready for the unique testing at the combine and build our bodies back up after the college season. Dave brought in a lot of former NFL players to talk with us about real issues—like the company we kept off the field and staying aware of the magnitude of the opportunity ahead of us.

Dave considered our tape and our game film as our GPAs and our combine scores as our SAT or ACT scores. He coached us hard, but it was what we needed! We even developed a rapport with the guys who were training there. It was like a little team of our own for a few weeks.

Dave had known me since I was 17 and was more like a big brother than a trainer—he knew exactly which buttons to push. He knew no matter what he programmed for me, I would do it. If he told me to jump, I would ask, "How high?" That is the relationship we have: He believes in me, and I trust in him.

> Dave brought in a lot of former NFL players to talk with us about real issues— like the company we kept off the field and staying aware of the magnitude of the opportunity ahead of us.

"You have to be satisfied with the man in the mirror," he said. "You've gotta be satisfied with the effort you gave. I never want people to experience regret."

I have no regrets.

FINDING THE RIGHT AGENT

The process to find an agent was unique. I forwarded the applications of all the potential agents to my mom and dad. All told, there were a lot to choose from. All through the season, we received pamphlets from the different agencies. They all had great pitches and glossy books full of their clients on NFL fields. But I really didn't want to think about an agent until after I was done with my college career.

My parents met with six of the biggest agencies in the country and

> The most important thing is to choose an agent you trust and enjoy being around.

narrowed it down to four. After the Rose Bowl, I met with those agents. Mom was extremely high on one of the guys, and I ended up going with Steve Caric, who had guided the careers of NFL stars like Steven Jackson and Drew Bennett. She was right about the Stanford decision, and she was right about the agent.

What I didn't understand when I was in college is that I had my boys with me every day, and we were all going through the same trials and tribulations. In the NFL, I suddenly didn't have anyone to talk to. The NFL is a league full of sole proprietors—every guy is his own little corporation. I needed someone to help me with the on-field trials I was facing. I could maybe talk to the general manager about what was going on, but having a great agent means having someone in my corner who *always* has my back.

Steve and I are more than agent and client; we're best friends. We talk on the phone all the time. Steve says he "represents clients as part of his family, focusing on trust, honesty, and loyalty to build lifelong relationships." I've found that to be the case.

People can get hung up on marketing when choosing an agent. If you produce on the football field, the marketing opportunities will come. The most important thing is to choose an agent you trust and enjoy being around.

THE COMBINE EXPERIENCE

Here's the deal with the NFL Scouting Combine in Indianapolis: it's a weird audition-type thing that requires you to get into peak condition for a unique workout just six weeks after the end of your college season. So your fingers are crushed, your legs are sore, and your body is beaten up, but you have to train for a very specific kind of track meet—and by that, I mean a track meet that is you against the clock on a slow piece of FieldTurf in Lucas Oil Stadium on a day in which it is invariably 20 degrees, gray, and sleeting.

Coming from the West Coast, I was at a severe disadvantage already because of the time change. I got into my hotel room in downtown Indianapolis and tried to sleep—but failed. I was too worked up about what I would put myself through in a matter of hours.

The analogy has already been drawn before, but the combine is like a cattle call. You get a number on your chest that is your number for the rest of the week. It's the number the organizers will use to herd you in and out of rooms with other groups of large, nervous men who are trying really hard to look larger (muscles, good!) and less nervous (nerves, bad!). You are issued a neon spandex—What's the word parents use for the thing they put on babies?—*onesie*. You'll wear the onesie for all your running, catching, jumping, and lifting drills. In it, you will feel a little, well, infantile, but you will put such thoughts out of your mind because you are focused (focus, good!).

> There is no feeling like that of parading in front of a roomful of grown men who are dressed while you're wearing underwear and they're scribbling things about you into little notebooks.

You won't wear it when you march across the stage in your underwear to be weighed and have your (ahem) hands measured. There is no feeling like that of parading in front of a roomful of grown men who are dressed while you're wearing underwear and they're scribbling things about you into little notebooks. They write things like "Zach is a little thin in the hips" or "Zach is cut high." Good times!

Height: 6'5"

Weight: 249 pounds

"Look, Mom, my arm is ten inches across!"

INTERVIEWS

That evening, I was stressed out because I had 20 formal team interviews, which essentially amount to one-on-several conversations with prospective teams. These take place in hotel rooms that are attached to Lucas Oil Stadium. You open the door *as* you're knocking (being assertive, good!), but you don't open it too fast because you don't want to look arrogant (bad!)—unless teams like a little "attitude" (good!). Firm handshakes and football-related banter abound among the men in team-logoed windbreakers.

> After you're done for the day, you go back to your hotel room and replay every conversation you had with every team, hoping you said the right things.

This is a good time to reassert that I actually did appreciate the process and all the interest that teams were taking in me. But the interviews kept me up late every night and made it hard to sleep. I tossed and turned, hoping I had given the right responses. I'm also a wildly introverted dude, so opening up conversationally was tough and draining. It may have worn me out more than the workout itself!

"Who's someone in the NFL you think you can compare yourself to?" a scout might ask. You try to come up with the right name, the very picture of toughness and pride and focus, and you always mention one of the top guys to play the position even if it couldn't be further from the truth. Tony Gonzales was a good one for me. He was a former basketball guy (like me)—but tough and a pro's pro.

In these meetings, the scouts might cue up a tape of your good plays or your bad plays or both and have you talk through them. They might put you on the whiteboard to draw up some coverages. They might ask whether you'd prefer to be a dog or a cat (spoiler: dog is always the right answer).

From there, it's across the street to the hospital on a series of elaborate cat-walks that keep you protected from the elements outside. The scouts take every MRI of every injury you've ever had, and then they push and poke and prod those injuries. They try to do everything they can so you perform your worst on the last day.

Finally, it's back into the onesie for the workouts themselves. Before you go out, you do pushups in the hallway to get a good pump on because if you have to wear the onesie, you might as well look good in it. The year I was there, I had to wear an Iron Man–esque monitor across my chest. Whenever my heart rate elevated, the scouts knew about it. Tony Stark has nothing on a prospective draft pick at the 2013 NFL Scouting Combine.

> The scouts take every MRI of every injury you've ever had, and then they push and poke and prod those injuries. They try to do everything they can so you perform your worst on the last day.

I didn't jump extremely well because I somehow missed some of the red, white, and blue tags you're supposed to slap at the top of the jump. My 40 wasn't great either. There was another guy in another team windbreaker making sure my hand was where it should be and left the turf exactly how it was supposed to. "But just relax, Zach," he said.

Relax in spite of all the NFL Network cameras and guys who hold your professional future in their hands. I think I ran a 4.7, which I wasn't thrilled with, but I crushed the on-field work, which is where you get to run routes and catch balls and do all the stuff that feels natural.

PRO DAY

I had my Pro Day at Stanford about three weeks later. Pro Days are just like the Scouting Combine—except without the plane flight and the Under Armour onesie and the cattle-call aspect. Pro Day took place on a sunny, perfect day in Palo Alto, with a few nights of great sleep in my own bed behind me and, best of all (sponsor shout-out ahead), with my Nike gear on!

Beforehand, I talked to my agent and my trainer and thought I could do better at the 40 and the jumps. I didn't worry about the bench or any of the agilities. I ran high 4.5s and jumped 35.5 inches after jumping 31.0 at the combine. Overall, I felt way more comfortable and in my element at Stanford. After Pro Days, most guys have a ton of visits and workouts. I only worked out with the Falcons and Eagles, which amounted to getting some team-issued swag and doing a lot of the same drills from the combine.

> I only worked out with the Falcons and Eagles, which amounted to getting some team-issued swag and doing a lot of the same drills I did at the Pro Day and Combine.

A note about those individual workouts: They can be a lot more tiring than a normal practice because (a) your adrenaline is jacked and (b) there's only one guy—you—running routes, with no rest. Ask a question or two between routes as a means of catching your breath.

I only had two local visits with the Raiders and 49ers. I didn't have a lot of background stuff they had to do their due diligence on, so those were pretty quick and easy. And I won't lie—I loved the idea of staying close to home in the Bay Area and playing for Coach Harbaugh, who was with the 49ers.

THE NFL DRAFT

I tend to be a pretty intense person, so draft day wasn't a fun, whimsical experience for me like it is for some other guys. I didn't throw a huge party, nor did I get on a boat and go fishing like perennial All-Pro and future Hall of Fame tackle Joe Thomas famously did. The draft, like a lot of things related to the NFL (including the combine), has become a massive, made-for-television spectacle with huge on-site crowds, celebrities reading the picks, and cameras everywhere. There are guys like Mel Kiper and Todd McShay, whose whole careers revolve around speculating about where certain guys are going to be drafted.

> Instead of celebrating or enjoying the draft, I sat there in silence and watched the whole first round come and go.

But instead of celebrating or enjoying any of it, I sat in silence and watched the whole first round come and go. When you're waiting to see where you're going to live and start your career, you live and die with every pick. The Bears were picking at 20, and I knew it was between offensive lineman Kyle Long (son of the legendary Howie Long) and myself. They took Long. Then I thought my next best shot would be the Texans at 26, though superstar receiver DeAndre Hopkins fell to them, and they grabbed him.

But my real dream at the time was to stay in the Bay Area and play for Harbaugh with the 49ers, which I thought was a distinct possibility. They had a pair of picks; however, they traded up to get safety Eric Reid.

I was all over the map emotionally after the first round. I was alternately crushed and hot. Intellectually, I knew I would get a chance to play in the NFL and that it would come soon, but I felt like all the work I'd done

> Looking back on it now, it's silly and a little sinful—seeking praise and validation from man and being so torn up when I didn't get it.

throughout my career was spinning down the drain because I didn't get the validation I was looking for.

Looking back on it now, it's silly and a little sinful—seeking praise and validation from man and being so torn up when I didn't get it. Everybody in the house was silent. Nobody knew what to say to me. In a football context, you're praised for your intensity, but it didn't do me any favors on draft night.

THE CALL

"Why don't we take a drive?" Julie suggested wisely. We hopped in the car and just drove around and talked. Finally, we ended up in a Krispy Kreme shop where we absolutely crushed a whole bunch of doughnuts. It was a legendary decision by my wife.

I played against former Oregon head coach Chip Kelly in college four times, and when I declared for the draft, he was the head coach of the Eagles. I met with him at the combine, and as I was leaving, I said, "Hopefully I'll see you soon."

"I hope I see you right after the draft," he replied. That kind of stuck in my head, and I had a feeling that if things broke a certain way, I might end up in Philly.

> At pick 35, I got a call from a Philly area code. It was Chip, saying, "We want you to be a Philadelphia Eagle." It was awesome.

The next day (Friday), I knew I was going to go early. At pick 35, I got a call from a Philly area code. It was Chip, saying, "We want you to be a Philadelphia Eagle." It was awesome. I'll never forget it. It's the phone call every kid dreams of getting, and I'm extremely grateful to Howie Roseman and Chip for believing in me.

Former Eagles Pro Bowl linebacker Jeremiah Trotter strode up to the podium with the commissioner to read the pick: "With the thirty-sixth pick in the 2013 NFL Draft, the Philadelphia Eagles select Zach Ertz, tight end, Stanford."

A LONG WAY TO PHILLY

And just like that, I was an Eagle. My highlight package played on-screen while I finished up the call. It was surreal to see myself in the way a fan might see me. They praised my route running, my ability to get off the line of scrimmage, and my capacity to track the ball in the air. They dinged me for my lack of elite deep speed and my in-line blocking. This would become a theme . . . but at the moment, I was an Eagle, and that's all that mattered.

The rest of that day is a blur. There was some celebrating at home, but then I only had a couple hours to throw some clothes in a bag and begin to realize that for the first time in my life, I would live someplace besides California. Some-

> Philly was famous for having a *tough* (but exceedingly loyal) fan and media base.

place new and challenging. Philadelphia is the city of Rocky and the Broad Street Bullies (hockey—the Flyers) and where Charles Barkley and Dr. J played for the Philadelphia 76ers. Football-wise, the tradition is rich as well, with players like Randall Cunningham, Seth Joyner, and Reggie White becoming legends in the old Veteran's Stadium. And Philly was famous for having a *tough* (but exceedingly loyal) fan and media base.

I'd have to say goodbye to Julie, and I was cognizant of the fact that I'd be saying goodbye for a long time when camp started, as she was still in college. For the first time in our relationship, we'd be living far apart. Julie actually wasn't there the day I got drafted, so I tried calling but couldn't get ahold of her. It turned out she was crying when she found out I was going all the way to Philadelphia. I said goodbye to my mom for the first extended period of my life.

In a weird way, I expected my life to *feel* different. But nobody stopped me in the airport. There was no celebration. I'm not sure what I expected—maybe some kind of transcendent feeling when I achieved my dream. But in reality, I was in the back row of the plane in a middle seat where, based on the smell, I'm pretty sure somebody threw up on the flight before mine.

WAR ROOM

It was a whirlwind. I landed in Philly and met a guy from the team who was holding a card with my name written on it. I hopped in the car and was driven through the city for the first time. The houses and buildings looked architecturally different from those in San Francisco. We drove over a large bridge and past the stadium that would become my workplace. Past the Rocky statue at the art museum. I tried to get my head around the fact that I'd be living here.

> I tried to get my head around the fact that I'd be living here.

We rolled up to the Eagles NovaCare Complex facility, which, like most NFL facilities, looks like it could be a new science building at a university, with lots of dark, brushed steel; glass; and the requisite photos of Eagles legends like Randall Cunningham and Donovan McNabb. My first moments at NovaCare were a whirlwind of "Hey, Zach Ertz, great to meet you" and "I'm really happy to be here."

I walked down a narrow hallway to the Eagles "war room," where prospects are listed on a huge wall. Head Coach Chip Kelly came out and gave me a big bro hug. "Where were you?" he asked.

"Home . . . California," I replied. The other side of the country. Chip was wearing a Nike pullover from a bowl game he'd coached in college. It's weird the stuff you remember.

STRESS CONFERENCE

It was all really exciting, but the thing is, I was secretly terrified of the press conference that would happen later that evening. When I was a kid, I saw a speech therapist for stuttering, and I was nervous about speaking in front of everyone—like red-faced, taking-deep-breaths-in-the-bathroom nervous. It was worse than what I felt like before any game.

> I was ready to stop talking and start playing football.

I was mumbling and stuttering over my words. I took these long pauses, and they actually moved my conference off to the side, away from the TV cameras. They called it short. I was exhausted and nervous and grateful that they had cut it. I was ready to stop talking and start playing football.

6

PHILADELPHIA STORY

The 2012 Eagles were 4–12, so there was a lot of room for improvement. The team's previous coach, Andy Reid, an NFL coaching legend, had just been fired, and the new coach, Chip Kelly, was right out of the college ranks. The Eagles already had tight end Brent Celek, an established star, so I wasn't really sure where I'd fit.

Moving to Philly was definitely an eye-opener. I was born in California and went to school close to home. If I needed to see family, I only had to drive 40 minutes. All of a sudden, I was 3,000 miles away, and my girlfriend was still in college at Santa Clara.

Both my mom and dad went to college in Pennsylvania, and they had some connections in Philly. One of my mom's friends suggested a safe, secure apartment complex that happened to be ten minutes from the NFL facility. I had a two-bedroom, three-bath apartment, which was probably too much real estate for me. I mean, when you're one guy living alone, how many bathrooms do you need?

My whole rookie year was a blur. From the moment I started my senior year in college, I began training for the combine. Then there was the NFL draft, minicamp, and then the real training camp. I felt like I had no breaks from football because I had been either playing it or training to play it for two years in a row. It was actually harder mentally than physically. I love football, but I think that to really love it well and to be ready for it mentally, you need some time away from it to let your body heal and your affection for it grow again.

I'm kind of a homebody by nature, so living by myself wasn't a huge deal. I didn't mind leaving the facility at night, grabbing some fast food, and then coming home to an empty apartment. But the food situation was the hardest thing.

In college, if you're hungry, you can simply walk into the meal room at the football building or in your dorm and get food. At my school, there were always all kinds of lean, healthy options—with none of the cleanup. In the NFL, however, there are days when the players are not eating every meal at the facility. That meant I was on my own for a few days a week, and I ate a lot of Chipotle!

COWORKERS, TEAMMATES, FRIENDS

Relationship-wise, that first year I spent a lot of time with offensive tackle Lane Johnson. Backup quarterback Matt Barkley actually lived in the same apartment complex as I did, and every now and then, we'd hang out together. Nick Foles was my closest friend, though, and he lived in the same complex as well. We have very similar personalities and enjoy doing the same things. We don't take ourselves too seriously, and we like to joke around. We've definitely matured a lot over the years in terms of football and our perspectives on the game.

Getting to know people during my rookie year was tough. Stanford's old NFL graduation rule was that you couldn't participate in the off-season program until your school year was over. My classes didn't end until June 12 because my college was on the quarter system. I missed most of the organized team activities in the spring, and as a result, I didn't know anyone besides the rookies when I got out there.

ACCLIMATION DAYS

I came in for training camp a few days early with the other rookies. The coaches call these "acclimation days." I walked into one of the first meetings and saw Michael Vick, and that's when it really hit me that I was in the NFL. I grew up playing as him in the Madden video games, and now he was my coworker! I also learned that he is one of the nicest guys ever. He had been through a lot, on and off the field, and by the time he got to Philly, there was a kind of calmness about him that I gravitated toward.

> I missed most of the organized team activities in the spring, and as a result, I didn't know anyone besides the rookies when I got out there.

There's nothing like being in a pro locker room for the first time as a rookie.

There were a lot of veterans on the team—grown men with wives and kids and lots of years in the league. That said, training camp was a bit of a shock for those guys. For the first time in 40 years, the Eagles actually had

> There's nothing like being in a pro locker room for the first time as a rookie.

camp in Philly. We rookies would sleep in a local hotel and take shuttle buses to the facility. In previous years, the Eagles had their training camp at Lehigh University, which is where my dad went to college.

Training camp is a mental and physical grind. The day usually starts around 6:00 a.m. with breakfast. After some eggs, oatmeal, and juice, it's off to the training room to treat any reported ailments or injuries. And since NFL teams report all their injuries, there's this old cliché: "You can't make the club in the tub"—meaning you can't improve and advance your career if you're stuck in the training room working out a sore calf. It's a great incentive to not tell the team about everything that's hurting you, especially as a rookie trying to prove your worth.

From there it's weight lifting, which is tough to do when you're bruised and sore from the previous day. Your body feels 100 years old during the first few reps, but then it starts to refortify itself, and you can feel the effects of the weights. It's important to not lose all the strength progress that you've made in the off-season.

> In a Chip Kelly camp, the tempo was always high . . . we were always in a hurry.

After weights, there's a general team meeting to kick off the day, then a special-teams meeting where the team watches the tape from the previous day's practice. The only guys who get out of this meeting are the quarterbacks; they go to a different room to do their own thing. After that, it's off to a positional meeting and then to the locker room to get ready for morning practice.

Typically, the first practice is lighter—maybe just helmets and shorts, not full pads—and is more of a mental thing. But in a Chip Kelly camp, the tempo was always high, regardless of whether it was morning or afternoon. Chip wanted us to run a lot of offensive plays, so we were always in a hurry.

One of the toughest moments mentally for me and many NFL players is the time before afternoon practice. I would be sitting in front of my locker, knowing I had to put my pads on and go out to do it again. Don't get me wrong—I love the game, but in those moments, I had to ignore the pain in my body and not listen to the voice in my head that was telling me to quit and walk away. Soon the shoulder pads, the green Riddell helmet with the Eagles wings, and the white jersey with "Ertz" sewn on the back would go on, and it was a short jog out to the field past some clapping fans.

Camp practices are intimate. There are fans along the sidelines. Parents are there with their kids, who line up for autographs afterward. It's such a cool thing to be a part of. Camp practices are also physical, and it's where you compete hard to distinguish yourself from the other guys at your position. For the first month, your teammates are also your competitors, but then as soon as the roster is set, it's like, "Okay, never mind, these guys are my friends, and we can stop trying to kill each other."

> For the first month, your teammates are also your competitors, but then as soon as the roster is set, it's like, "Okay, never mind, these guys are my friends, and we can stop trying to kill each other."

THE CHIP KELLY TACKLING DRILL

In one of my first padded training camp practices, we ran the Chip Kelly tackling drill. It's really simple: Tight ends (TEs) and outside

> You're trying not to fall asleep even though you're perpetually nervous.

linebackers (OLBs) line up five yards apart. One guy has the ball, and the other guy has to stop him. We were getting blasted by these OLBs, grown men like Trent Cole and Conner Barwin, who weren't going to let a rookie TE run through them. Trent was an animal, and at the time, he was the Eagles all-time sack leader. He wore number 58, had these tribal tattoos all over his huge biceps, and wore a visor on his helmet. In one rep I had against Trent, he picked me up and dumped me on the ground—just planted me! I separated my shoulder, and we never did that drill again.

On a typical camp day, there's a dinner and then another long positional meeting in the evening. That last meeting is a tough one—you're in a dark, air-conditioned film room after a long day of banging and running, and you're staring at a screen watching the stuff you lived through just a few hours before. You're looking for anything you can use the next day—a tweak to your stance, an imbalance in your foot or hand placement, an adjusted route, anything. More important, you're trying not to fall asleep even though you're perpetually nervous.

After the meeting, I would take the shuttle bus back to the hotel, put in a sleepy call to my girlfriend or parents, and then try (often in vain) to drift off to sleep with each of that day's reps fresh in my mind. Then rinse and repeat the whole process the next day. And the day after that.

The evening after I injured my shoulder was a little different. I called Julie and my agent and had a bunch of treatment on it, already worrying about the time and reps I was going to lose in the process. My shoulder was really sore, but I was determined not to let it interfere with practice or my first preseason game against the Patriots. I imagined putting on an NFL game uniform for the first time and seeing live game action and realized that I had been living almost exclusively for that moment.

In a way, that drill was indicative of Chip's tenure with the Eagles. Chip meant well, but a few things from his college career had carried over into his NFL coaching style, which didn't sit well with a lot of the players. He tried to micromanage them and didn't give them the freedom to understand what he was trying to do and navigate their way through it. Still, it was stunning that first year to be around such talented guys. DeSean Jackson is still the fastest player I've ever played with. Watching LeSean McCoy in games was unbelievable. He led the league in rushing that year.

We used to do a one-on-one route-running exercise with the TEs and OLBs alternating between run blocking, pass protection, and route running. Trent (Cole) and Connor (Barwin) were two veterans that summer, and there weren't many victories on my end of the drill. Those guys simply weren't going to be blocked by a rookie TE. Despite my failures, my desire to succeed continued to grow. My attitude was "Let's get a victory today." I had to adjust my mind-set and recognize my own small wins so I wouldn't get too down on myself.

> "Let's get a victory today."

OUT OF SIGHT, OUT OF MIND

I learned the culture around injuries in the NFL very early on: if you're not on the field, you're out of sight, out of mind. So I was rushing to get back after my shoulder injury from the tackling drill because there was no way I was going to miss our first preseason game.

Mentally, I had all the normal rookie-year stuff going on as well. I had come in at a high draft pick, and I expected to play a ton for this city, where people loved football and knew everything about the team. But in my case, the best TE in the history of the franchise was still on the team. Brent Celek was a great run blocker. His receiving had waned a little bit, but Chip wanted the team to run the ball, and whoever was the best run blocker was going to be on the field.

My role was restricted to third-down tries and two-minute drills. I had come in with high hopes, and it wasn't easy to spend that much time sitting on the bench. There were many days when I felt like I wanted to get out of there, but of course I didn't (and couldn't) say anything to the team. I wasn't complaining to Michael Vick about playing time—that's just not what you do.

> It wasn't easy to spend that much time sitting on the bench.

I expressed those kinds of thoughts to my agent, who said he would talk to the general manager (GM). The GM's message was that I needed to work on my run blocking, and that's what I did. There were flashes of good, fun games where I got to play a lot, but the inconsistency was killing me. I was living and dying with every play and snap. Thinking about it in bed. Not sleeping.

FIRST PRESEASON GAME

I'd separated my shoulder in that tackling drill three days before, but there was no way I was missing this. We played the Patriots at home in our first preseason game, and nothing was going to stop me from putting on my uniform and running out of the giant Eagles tunnel through the smoke.

I didn't play a lot in the first quarter and only had a few catches at the end of the first half. At halftime, my coach told me, "No more; you're done." Oftentimes I find that I'm asking the coaches to keep me in preseason games so I can get into a flow. Sometimes I tell them, "My caffeine hasn't even kicked in yet." That first game of my rookie season, I wanted to stay in because I had so much more to work on.

I didn't have a great blocking game. At the beginning, blocking in the NFL wasn't easy, and it was definitely the thing keeping me off the field. DeSean Jackson had a 70-yard touchdown that day, and the whole offense played well. There was a lot of optimism heading into the regular season.

7

SUDDENLY RICH

Growing up, I understood the value of a dollar. I knew my mom was struggling financially after the divorce, and I didn't want to ask her for money. I was a Catholic Youth Organization ref in high school to make a few bucks for gas and food. I feel like when I got to the NFL, I didn't "feel" the money right away. My wife grew up in a similar financial situation, and we're fortunate to be where we are now. But I don't feel markedly different from anybody else. Our sports are our jobs, and there has to be some level of compensation.

The average NFL career lasts only three years, so young players feel as if people are often telling them, "Don't spend *any* money." I saved it all. I ended up leasing a nice Audi A7, my dream car at the time, but I turned it back in when I got a car deal in Philly. I don't even own a car now. Life is funny

> I paid off all my mom's debt with my second contract.

that way. Now that I can afford to buy a nice car, my sponsors give me one to drive around for free.

I paid off all my mom's debt with my second contract, which was a really special thing for both of us, given how much she struggled with raising my brothers and me on her own. Now I got to alleviate the stress she felt from managing everything on her own. It was huge for her, and I was glad to be able to give back.

AUTOGRAPHS, APPEARANCES, AND MARKETING OFFERS

In addition to the standard player contract, there were other opportunities to make income off the field. When I got drafted, I immediately got a rookie player card deal and signed a ton of autographs for that. I earned several bucks per signature, which I thought was the best thing in the world. I was getting paid to write my name on my card with my picture on it!

> Under Armour offered more money, but I was always going to go with Nike—that was the brand.

I also got a shoe contract deal and had to decide whether to go with Nike, Adidas, or Under Armour. My college, Stanford, was a Nike school, and Nike was always the cool brand. They had Michael Jordan and my favorite athlete growing up, Kobe Bryant. Under Armour offered more money, but I was always going to go with Nike—that was the brand.

Nike gave me a website password to all their athletes, which works almost like a gift card allotment. It's pretty cool to give the code to my brothers on their birthdays. They've bought more stuff over the years than I have.

After my third year, I started getting more and more marketing offers. I did some one-off signings, and there were a lot of opportunities to make appearances here and there on behalf of companies. It's humbling that people are willing to pay me just to show up and chat. I'm very aware that this stage of my life won't last forever, but at the same time, I want to spend time investing in my marriage and my family, not just chasing after money.

MONDAY NIGHT WITH THE REDSKINS

On opening weekend in 2013, the Eagles would be unveiling Chip's new offense against a divisional opponent on Monday Night Football at FedEx Field in Landover, Maryland. Not too shabby. It hit me all at once, and I thought, "Dang, I'm really in the NFL, pulling on the white Eagles jersey, running out of the tunnel to the boos of a divisional crowd!" Somewhere, the Monday Night Football song was playing, and there was a highlight package with my team in it.

> The term "run-pass option" (RPO) has become a vogue thing the last couple of years, but we were calling them all the time that first season with Chip.

In that offense, I didn't know when or how I was going to be involved. Nobody really knew who was going to get the ball, but I didn't care. I was just so excited to be in the NFL and play in a game. We marched the ball right down the field on the first drive, with Michael Vick doing surgery at quarterback, but the drive was derailed by a weird defensive score on a batted pass that was determined to be a lateral.

We ran almost 70 plays in the first half. We were rolling, and for a while it felt like we were going to take over the league. What was crazy about that game—the first half especially—was how fast we were playing. It seemed like we were wearing the Redskins and their fans out, literally and figuratively. In that game, there were no pauses. There was a two-play sequence where DeSean Jackson smoked the coverage, using his speed to motor through the defense, and then LeSean McCoy gashed them seconds later on a zone read. It felt like we'd never slow down.

The term "run-pass option" (RPO) has become a vogue thing the last couple of years, but we were calling them all the time that first season with Chip. On LeSean's zone read, we had a pop pass called to Brent Celek too, if Vick had wanted to take the option.

> I was relieved to be on the stat sheet and excited to be a part of the offense.

My first NFL play came in the middle of the first quarter. I was lined up wide at the top of the formation in single coverage. I ran a deep post, which meant I ran as fast as I could and then planted toward the goal post. The ball was in the air, heading for my back shoulder, so I dove and twisted for it—and almost made the catch.

After that play, Chip was going nuts on the sideline, waving his arm for us to hurry up. I ran back to the line of scrimmage, and the next ball came my way as well. Vick took some pressure, and I dragged across the formation. The defensive back jumped on my back right before the pass got there, and I tumbled to the ground, bobbling the ball. We couldn't convert.

Thankfully, our defense played out of their minds in that first quarter, forcing a safety, a fumble, and an interception.

MY FIRST NFL CATCH

I made my first NFL catch toward the end of the quarter. I lined up in line on the left side of the formation and ran a little pop pass underneath the

Redskins' deep zone drops. I cradled the ball to my chest and rolled for a first down. One catch for 11 yards. The first of many. I was just relieved to be on the stat sheet and excited to be a part of the offense this early.

We ended up winning the game 33–27. I finished the game with the one catch.

People forget how good DeSean Jackson was that season. He finished with 82 catches for more than 1,300 yards, and it seemed like he was virtually unstoppable at the beginning of 2013. Still, Chip Kelly was a firm believer in his system over the players. His big thing was going as fast as possible. He didn't even care about the execution of plays.

We have a saying now under Doug Pederson: "Execution fuels emotion." The better your execution, the more enjoyment you're going to experience. I think you have to be able to scheme for certain guys. It was almost bizarre how little of a playbook we had with Chip. We really only ran seven or eight plays. The offense I played at Stanford was way more complex.

OUR HOME OPENER AGAINST THE CHARGERS

We had our home opener the next week. San Diego came to town on a warm, sunny, idyllic day in Philly. Early in the second half, on a Chargers possession, their wideout Malcolm Floyd went up for a ball and got wedged between two Eagles tacklers. There was nothing dirty about it, but Malcolm was laid out, immobile, on the field, and the paramedics had to carry him off on a backboard. Stuff like that is a scary reminder of the violence in the sport I play. Sometimes it's hard to shake it off and keep playing.

I got involved in the third quarter when Vick hit me on a deep crossing route off a play-action. I suddenly found myself with the ball, running free through the secondary, and it felt great! The NFL never feels easy, but at that moment, I felt like I belonged. I knew I could make plays downfield in the league. I added another stat in the fourth quarter on a little flat pass to the right side that I was able to take up the sideline for 20 yards.

MY FIRST NFL START—DENVER

I got my first start in Week 4 at Denver. In our offense at the time, "starting" wasn't a huge deal—it was just based on what personnel package was on the field for the first snap. I could not breathe in that stadium, and their future Hall of Fame quarterback Peyton Manning didn't have a ball hit the ground the whole day.

> I got to share a field with those legendary people, and I kept thinking, "What the heck, how did I get here?"

During my rookie year, I felt like nobody knew who I was, so I didn't go out of my way to interact with a star like Peyton. I just watched him from afar, but we made him look too good that day. Overall, that first year I got to share a field with those legendary people, and I kept thinking, "What the heck, how did I get here?"

Denver scored on a blocked punt, a kick return, and a bunch of Peyton Manning touchdown passes. They absolutely wore us out.

BACK TO THE BAY—OAKLAND

In Week 9, we got to travel to Oakland, California, to play the Raiders. Playing the Raiders on the road is wild because the fans paint themselves black and silver, scream obscenities at you during warm-ups, and often throw things. Somebody was dressed in a full Raider uniform with a chain-mail helmet and spikes coming out of the shoulder pads. It's a passionate fan base and a fun place to play.

Around 20 of my family members and friends from the Bay Area came to the game to see me. I also got to hang out with Julie that Saturday night. The game itself was almost like a fairytale—everything we did worked! We only ran about four or five different run plays, and our center, Jason Kelce, pulled on most of them. This means that as soon as he snapped the ball, he got to the perimeter and ran interference for LeSean or Bryce Brown. Kelce is a freak athlete and is probably faster than half the tight ends in the league. No exaggeration. He is also incredible at blocking in space.

The game was even more fun because I had my best receiving day of the season up to that point, catching five balls for 42 yards and my first NFL score.

A lot has changed in the NFL since that game. For one, Oakland's starting quarterback was Terrelle Pryor, who is now a wide receiver in the league. Legendary NFL defensive back Charles Woodson, a lock for the Hall of Fame, was still playing in their secondary.

MY FIRST NFL TOUCHDOWN

It was really special catching a touchdown from my good buddy Nick Foles, who absolutely went off in the Oakland game. Nick threw for more than 400 yards and seven touchdowns, which tied an NFL record. Nick and I were on the same page in all phases. I almost scored in the first quarter when he found me over the middle on a stop route underneath the Raiders' zone. I felt comfortable and in a great rhythm right away.

I scored my first NFL touchdown on a corner route near the end of the first half. Like in most formations that year, I was flexed out in the slot to the top of

> I had my best receiving day of the season up to that point, catching five balls for 42 yards and my first NFL score.

the formation. I ran about 12 yards, stuck my foot in the ground, and broke for the back corner. I was wide open, and Nick put the ball right on me. He was scrambling, and I was thrilled that he found me. Nick and I were room-mates on the road and hung out all the time, so we kind of shared a brain. I caught the pass, and it was just pure joy—pure satisfaction—which was multiplied by seeing all my family and friends after the game.

THE CARDINALS

The week before our road game against the Arizona Cardinals, Nick was named the starting quarterback. It's not like it is in the movies. As Nick said, nobody cried, and there was no big speech. Chip just called both Nick and Michael Vick into his office and said, "Nick you're the one; Mike, you're the two." And that was it. Nothing changed about Nick's approach, which is the great thing about him.

> Michael Vick was the consummate pro, helping Nick Foles in practice and on the sidelines in games.

The great thing about the situation in general—and a real learning moment for me as a person—was how great Mike was to Nick. He was the consum-mate pro, helping Nick in practice and on the sidelines in games. This is a guy who is an NFL superstar and a legend in the league, and he was a great person through a situation that could have been really awkward. It's really a testament to both those guys.

Sometimes on the sidelines, Mike would talk about what he was see-ing on the field (helpful), but sometimes when Nick was jittery, they'd just talk about things outside of football, and that would calm Nick down (even more helpful). That's a side of the game—and a side of Mike—that most people don't see. It was great for Nick and me to have an older player to look up to like that. Nick talked about what a blessing it was to be with the Eagles. I knew what he was talking about in a general sense, but at the time, I wasn't a believer yet.

But at the end of the day, Nick knew that his job was to win.

I knew going into the game against the Cardinals that I was going to be heavily involved in the offense. I had a great week of practice catching the ball and was excited.

MY PREGAME

Back then, Nick and I had a pregame routine where he would go out and just *launch* the ball. Nothing scripted, nothing super intense—we were just playing backyard football. We had a lot of fun with it, and it also improved our chemistry. So before the game against the Cardinals, I drove to the stadium and FaceTimed with Julie, as was customary. She told me to go out and dominate, as she always did. Once I got there, I took off my suit (all business on Sunday) and pulled on a pair of Eagles workout shorts and a T-shirt. I got my ankles taped and went out to throw and look at the stadium with Nick.

> The stadiums in the NFL almost look even more impressive when they're empty.

In those kinds of pregame moments, the players are allowed to soak it all in. The stadiums in the NFL almost look even more impressive when they're empty. There are a few early arriving fans there—real die hards—and you get a chance to sign some autographs and visit with them. Then you walk the field a little and get a sense for how the grass feels under your cleats. After that, I would do some jogging and then play backyard football with

Nick. The camera crews would be setting up, and the stands would gradually fill with people.

UNSTOPPABLE

The Cardinals game was probably the most fun I had playing football my rookie year. We were in our black jerseys on another picture-perfect East Coast football day. I started the game on the field, and it was the first time as a pro that I felt like the defense couldn't stop me.

> It was the first time as a pro that I felt like the defense couldn't stop me.

On the first drive of the game, I scored a touchdown on a fake toss to the left and a bootleg to the right. The whole defense had chased LeSean because of how effective our run game had been. It was Nick's seventeenth touchdown pass, with no interceptions on the season. As soon as I caught the ball and knew I was safe in the end zone, I pointed up into the stands at Julie and my mom. I even pulled out the Hunger Games celebration.

I had a huge 22-yard catch a couple of drives later. I was at the bottom of the formation, out wide, and we had a height advantage on the defensive back. Nick put the ball nice and high and out in front of me—just like in our pregame warm-up. I jumped up and grabbed it with my fingertips.

Like I said before, this was the first time I really felt unstoppable in the NFL. In the third quarter, I beat an Arizona offensive linebacker in man coverage from the slot. Nick hit me for 16 yards and a first down. I was really getting to show what I could do in a pro game, which was fun. We capped the drive with a skinny post in the end zone for the touchdown. What a blast—especially at home!

THE VIKINGS AND MY BEST CATCH

The other memorable game from my rookie year took place against the Vikings. We played them in their place, at Mall of America Field. Nick was on an absolutely blistering pace coming in, leading the league in QB rating at 120.1, with 20 touchdowns and only one interception.

Minnesota was scoring a ton of points, so the game plan shifted to focus on the pass. Whenever there was a lot of passing, I was involved a lot, which made for a fun game. This was another instance when I felt like the other team couldn't stop me.

One added bonus was that my coaches were starting to trust me as an in-line blocker. On one play in the third quarter, I found myself blocking the Vikings' All-Pro defensive end Jared Allen. Jared had a motor that never quit. LeSean went the "wrong" way on the play, but he was still able to pick up a first down and a drive that would end up in a bomb to DeSean Jackson in the end zone. Blocking for LeSean, I knew I had to sustain my block because he had such great vision, and the ball could come from anywhere.

My high point came at the very end of the third quarter, when I had a one-handed catch in the back of the end zone that is still to this day one of my best catches. I was lined up in the slot and ran a little stutter fade against Vikings safety Andrew Sendejo. Nick really laid the ball out there. I reached my hand out as far as I could, and the ball settled right into my palm.

> Now I trust in the Lord, and I trust the coaches to do their jobs.

I learned a lot my rookie year. When you're young, you press a lot more. Sometimes I'd try to make the game plans more about me than about the team. Now I trust in the Lord, and I trust the coaches to do their jobs. I go into the games and just try to have fun with the guys rather than focus on catches and yards. Knowing Christ has made my Sundays a lot more joyful.

Going into the off-season after that rookie year, though, I knew there were a few major things I'd need to work on if I was going to become one of the best in the league. And they were things that, at face value, had nothing to do with one another.

8

STUTTER STEP

Today as I sit down to write, I'm coming off a marathon three-hour lifting session in the gym. It was one of my first intense lifts of the off-season. My goal is to get my body feeling good again, so I went for high reps, high volume—four sets of ten on bench, eight sets of ten on rows. I want to build my body back and find ways to improve from last year. I feel better now going into year seven than I did going into year three.

I work with my strength coach from Stanford because we achieved a lot together when I was in college and have had so much success together now that I'm in the NFL. He knows what I need to do to maintain a football-specific workout plan.

Now that I'm a professional football player, there aren't a ton of overall strength gains I'm going to make, but ensuring everything is efficient and healthy is our top priority. He helps me mentally with the way we approach things. "The price always increases," he texted me before the workout. "You can't do the same thing over and over again and expect people not to catch up."

I love it—I feel like I've been given a unique and special opportunity each day I get to play football professionally. Going to work is still fun. I love grinding. I love proving to myself that I can be one of the best to ever do something. When it's all said and done, I want to be able to say, "Hey, I have no regrets, and I wouldn't change a dang thing."

> I love proving to myself that I can be one of the best to ever do something.

As I'm recovering from the workout, I learn that Jason Witten is coming out of retirement to play with the Dallas Cowboys. Witten is 36 years old and has put together a Hall of Fame career with the Cowboys. He's played his whole career with the same team, which is a goal of mine. He's a great guy. I loved watching him on and off the field because his class and preparation were second to none. And it's been interesting to watch him age as a tight end. He's not as explosive as he once was, but his game has adapted, and he's a complete pro who can still block well in line and get open.

I'm fascinated by guys like Witten and Antonio Gates, and I study them. They remind me of late-career Michael Jordan, who learned how to post up and developed a fadeaway jumper so he could stay competitive and relevant in the league. Witten is also an accomplished public speaker, which is honestly something that has always been a struggle for me. I feel so comfortable and confident in my body as an athlete, but the opposite has been true for me as a speaker.

OUT OF MY COMFORT ZONE

I had a stutter when I was young. I had to go to a speech therapist in elementary school to overcome it. I was really insecure about talking in front of the class and reading in front of people. I hated public speaking. I would get red, sweaty, shaky, and nauseous. I absolutely avoided it. I would ask my teachers for alternate assignments when they wanted the students to give speeches or read reports out loud.

With the job I have now, I have to talk to the media all the time. In my early Eagles interviews, I was nervous and stuttering. They actually cut my first press conference short because I was so uncomfortable. It's not something I would say I'm ever going to overcome, and I still struggle with it to this day. Sometimes my brain just works faster than my mouth can get the words out.

Two or three years ago, I had to hire a speech coach in Los Angeles to help me through it. It was not unlike working with Hudson Houck on my blocking after my second season in the pros. I would drive to his office feeling a little nervous, unsure of myself, and out of my element. Instead of a football field, it was me and the speech coach in his office, where I would practice speaking into a camera. Thankfully he was kind and patient!

He opened my eyes to how fast I was speaking. I felt like I was talking slowly, but when he played the recording back to me, I realized I was speaking a million words a minute. He told me it was okay to take a deep breath and understand my thoughts before trying to articulate them.

Any time I give a big speech now, especially regarding my faith, I pray beforehand that God will allow His Spirit to fill me and that whatever comes out will glorify Him. I feel like that allows me to relax and do my best.

When I was younger, I was afraid the media would distort the words I said in an interview in order to generate a story.

> I feel so comfortable and confident in my body as an athlete, but the opposite has been true for me as a speaker.

> If you put a lot of stock in what these people are saying about you, it's going to eat you up inside, and you're not going to last.

But now with some maturity, I realize they have a job to do—just like me. Journalism is so competitive, and sometimes they have to write stories they don't want to write. But if you put a lot of stock in what these people are saying about you, it's going to eat you up inside, and you're not going to last. I've seen it absolutely destroy guys in the league. The Bible talks about the "fear of man," and it's alive and well in the NFL, even though we all look pretty invincible on TV.

OFF-SEASON

Early in my career, I had a mentor in Palo Alto approach me in the off-season and invite me to dinner with Hall of Fame safety Ronnie Lott, who had won several Super Bowls with the San Francisco 49ers. It was a golden opportunity to get inside the mind of a legend.

"What are your goals?" Ronnie asked that night. I remember he looked like he could still play.

"I want to go to the Pro Bowl and be All-Pro," I replied.

"What's keeping you from that?" he asked.

"Playing time. I'm only on the field 50 percent of the time."

"Why's that?" he asked. He already knew the answer, and so did I: run blocking. He challenged me to find ways around the NFL off-season rules, which prohibit you from working with coaches at the beginning of the off-season.

I called my position coach and said I wanted to work with an offensive-line coach on my blocking. Chip Kelly told me about a guy named Hudson

Houck, a legendary line coach for the Cowboys who was working with linemen in San Diego on a freelance basis. Continuing my tradition of following great players, I told Darren Sproles I was going to follow him around in the off-season to work out with him and see how he handled himself off the field.

Those were the longest days. I paid out of pocket, and it was not cheap. Hudson had an unbelievable pedigree, having coached players like Larry Allen, Erik Williams, and Nate Newton on the Cowboy dynasty teams from the '90s. He was in his seventies when I met him, but he had an innate understanding of blocking, balance, and leverage.

I was willing to do whatever it took to be a complete tight end.

At Stanford, we prided ourselves on being a physical run-blocking team. But I was the "move" tight end—I blocked in space, but I wasn't a great hand-in-the-ground tight end. These were skills I needed Hudson to develop in me on the fly because I was willing to do whatever it took to be a complete tight end. And I was willing to pay a premium for them!

OLD SCHOOL

Hudson's training methods were old school. We had a medicine ball and a blocking pad—that's it. While we worked on our blocks, Hudson had someone hold the bag so he could watch us. A lot of times, I wouldn't engage my hips, which meant that I'd lean too much, get overextended, and get thrown. It was all about rolling my hips at the start of the contact.

I worked for hours during that off-season, drill after drill after drill, because I wanted to be on the field. I think it's unique to go outside the facility for training, but it makes sense in the NFL because there's not a lot

> In almost every phase of life, you have to come up with a plan to address your weaknesses.

of time spent on the basics like blocking and route running. In almost every phase of life, you have to come up with a plan to address your weaknesses.

In every scenario, you're going to be outmatched as a tight end. Safeties are going to be faster, and defensive ends are going to be bigger and stronger (like DeMarcus Lawrence from the Cowboys, who is so relentless, so strong. His motor is unwavering). As a result, our technique has to be on point and flawless. If you overemphasize the run game during the season, you're not going to be a good route runner and pass catcher. Sometimes you have to look elsewhere to address your weaknesses.

FRIENDSHIPS: QUALITY OVER QUANTITY

Relationally, offensive tackle Lane Johnson was my friend on and off the field, and he was one of the funniest guys on the Eagles. Lane is very "Oklahoma" and pure comedy all the time. He and I were dealing with a lot of similar pressures those first couple years. LeSean McCoy was super loquacious, always talking smack to everyone. Jason Kelce is hilarious. The offensive linemen are a very special group of people—they're some of the smartest guys on the team, usually the funniest, and have to be in tune. They do their own thing and have their own culture, but hanging out with them is sort of like visiting a different

> The offensive linemen are a very special group of people—they're some of the smartest guys on the team, usually the funniest, and have to be in tune.

country. You can enjoy it, but it requires a lot of time to get to know the rules and customs.

I'm heavily invested in the few friendships I have, but I don't have a ton of friends, which may be a weird thing to admit! It was the same in high school and college. I look for people who are able to be vulnerable and who have similar values. People gravitate toward those who are like them, but I also don't like to be wary of people who are different. I ultimately look for someone who's going to be invested in me as a person and not just a player.

> Year by year, it takes a village to keep me on the field.

There are some natural divisions in any locker room based on age and how you grew up. There are always going to be people who hang out together and those who don't. That said, the locker rooms we've had in Philly have been very inclusive, and people are very understanding. It's been amazing. Even though the other players might be focused on different things, we have a bond and a kinship and mutual respect.

I think it's unique playing a sport where 53 guys—no matter how they were raised—come together to achieve the same goal. You have to learn about other people's backgrounds, but everybody loves the game. It's a melting pot. You find ways to grow together, believe together, and love each other.

MY SUPPORT SYSTEM

There are so many people in Philly who have helped me along the way. Year by year, it takes a village to keep me on the field. My mom has always been very supportive. She's involved in running our foundation and also all the day-to-day mom things. I still call her when I need her. We have an amazing relationship. My wife and my mom get along fantastically, which I don't take for granted—it's a huge blessing!

Julie and I lean heavily on our pastor and his wife at Connect Church, which is based in Cherry Hill. He's a really special guy who played football at Tennessee and Richmond and can relate to the unique demands I face as a football player. He loves the Lord and loves Jesus. He baptized me the day before he officiated our wedding. He's just someone who loves and understands us and wants to see us succeed. I know he's always speaking from a place of scriptural truth and not just his own feelings. I need that. He also understands the pressures that Julie and I deal with, like having to be apart for so long.

We have a sign in our home with text from Luke 6:46-48, which is about building your house on a strong foundation—and that foundation is Christ. It reads:

> Why do you call me "Lord, Lord," and not do what I tell you?
>
> Everyone who comes to me and hears my words and does them, I will show you what he is like: he is like a man building a house, who dug deep and laid the foundation on the rock. And when a flood arose, the stream broke against that house and could not shake it, because it had been well built.

We try to build our relationship on the Word and love and not on anything superficial like money, influence, or sports. If our individual relationships with the Lord are messed up, our relationship with each other is going to be messed up.

Julie is in Nashville as I write this, playing pro soccer. I miss her like crazy. We talk every day, and we have to, otherwise we'll both go insane. Texting and FaceTime are huge for us. We have to be in constant communication to support each other.

YEAR TWO

I was a bigger part of the offense in 2014—in part because my blocking, while still a work in progress, was slowly improving. It was year two for Chip, and we had turned a lot of heads with our offense in 2013. Our quarterback, Nick Foles, was coming off an unbelievable year. He threw 27 touchdowns with only two picks and went to the Pro Bowl. Everyone had high expectations for us. Unfortunately, 2014 would be a season of injuries and challenges for Nick and lots of emotional ups and downs for me.

> The feeling is different when you're not a rookie . . . You're expected to produce, and I put a lot of pressure on myself in that regard.

Our personnel had changed some on offense, with DeSean Jackson leaving for the Redskins. I was going to be counted on to fill some of his production in our scheme, and that fact lived in the back of my mind throughout the season. The feeling is different when you're not a rookie. Your "grace period" of adjusting to the pro game is over. You're expected to produce, and I put a lot of pressure on myself in that regard.

We started with a big win against Jacksonville at home. I played against my old college buddy Toby Gerhart, who was the starting running back for Jacksonville. I had our first catch of the season on a seamer from Nick. It was the kind of play we had made a living on toward the end of the previous season. I lined up in the slot, made a little outside move and then a little inside move on a safety playing a short zone. First down!

I scored on a similar play in the third quarter. We were 25 yards out, and I ran right up the middle of the field, splitting the two high safeties. Nick floated the ball up there, and I came down with it right on the goal line. Touchdown! Emphatic spike! We came from behind to win the game 34–17.

BREAKTHROUGH OR BREAKDOWN?

We beat the Redskins 37–34 in Week 3. We threw the ball a ton, but I only had two catches. Jordan Matthews and Jeremy Maclin both did a great job, catching eight balls apiece. I'm not going to lie, though, it was tough to not be super involved.

> I actually broke down crying, which could be seen as a sign of weakness but could also be seen as a sign of how much it mattered to me.

Despite having some good games and high points, I was a disaster emotionally. I wasn't sleeping. That season was full of ups and downs. Nothing demonstrated this more than having the Eagles record for catches at 15 toward the end of the season but catching no balls against the Texans and barely playing. I'm sure people thought I was a bad teammate at the time. After the Texans game, I asked the tight ends coach, "What's going on? I feel like I have to be perfect in order to play." I felt like no matter how much work I put in, nothing would change.

The tight ends coach for the Eagles at the time was Ted Williams, who had been a position coach in the organization for 20 years. He was grizzled and old school, and I'm sure he'd seen it all, so my outburst didn't faze him.

I actually broke down crying, which could be seen as a sign of weakness but could also be seen as a sign of how much it mattered to me—because it mattered a ton! I was under a tremendous amount of pressure. I was grabbing onto my identity as a player, and at that time, I had no identity in Christ to level me out. It got to the point where I was questioning my future in

Philadelphia. Julie encouraged me to keep pushing and assured me that I'd eventually be great. It was not easy that year.

Coach Williams's message that day was pretty standard and pretty consistent with what you'd expect to hear in the NFL: Be a better teammate. Keep grinding. It will get better.

In addition to my drama, our quarterback Nick was going through his own—missing significant time with another injury.

MARK SANCHEZ

There was no upside to Nick getting hurt, but it did give me a chance to play with Mark Sanchez, who took over at quarterback. Mark had been a highly touted first-round pick of the New York Jets, and he came into the league with a lot of fanfare. Mark had a big personality, which fans got to see on HBO's *Hard Knocks*. I enjoyed him, as did the rest of the guys. We respected him for how hard he worked. On top of that, Mark and I really connected in a big game against the Redskins late in the season.

I had a whopping 15 catches for 115 yards. It was wild! We couldn't stop the Redskins on offense, and they couldn't stop us. The game got going, and the catches just kept adding up. I started cramping up in the second half, and Darren Sproles was like, "C'mon, Z, I need you!"

> There's only one team that can be happy at the end of the year.

That year was an emotional roller coaster for me. The Eagles ended up 10–6 and didn't make the playoffs. There's only one team that can be happy at the end of the year, after all. But I used the off-season that year to get away and get my head right. I needed some time outside the city to refocus on the people in my life who mattered most.

9

WHOLE FOODS, WHOLE PERSON

I'm late getting to the computer today because of an emergency, last-second Whole Foods run for Julie, who is returning home tonight for a few days of downtime during her pro soccer season. It's cool grocery shopping here in Philly. A lot of people want to chat and take pictures with me. I'm under a lot of pressure to select the perfectly curated hipster foods, sold by unbelievably happy and fashionable people. I hope I come through in crunch time!

Similarly, our current head coach, Doug Pederson, felt pressure when he took over for Chip Kelly after the 2015 season. Doug's route to the Eagles head coaching job was circuitous, to say the least. He played quarterback for the Miami Dolphins, the New York / New Jersey Knights (World League of American Football), the Carolina Panthers, the Miami Dolphins, the Rhein Fire (NFL Europe), the Dolphins again, the Green Bay Packers, the Eagles, the Cleveland Browns, and then (finally) the Eagles again. In 2008, he was a high school coach, and then, after a couple of stops as an assistant in the league, he was named our head coach. Philosophically, Doug is all about going 1–0 every single week, and that's the mentality we've had.

FREE TO BE MYSELF

When Doug came in, he told us, "I'm gonna give you the freedom and the ability to police yourselves—until somebody else has to step in." That declaration sat well with the guys. Doug has an innate sense for when to give someone space and when to push back. He wants our personalities to show through, and he wants us to play with confidence and swagger.

> Doug is all about going 1–0 every single week.

Getting a new coach didn't change much for me, but I felt more confident and free to be myself. We're still about the team, but if individuals get hyped, we all get hyped. We've got a great group of veteran guys—everybody gets each other going, and it's definitely a fun group.

Chip's practices were all about seeing how many plays we could run. There are still plays we run from the Chip era that work well for us, but Doug believes technique is the most important thing. He says, "Execution is the only way to win in this league." Our focus now is on executing at a high level.

In the beginning, nobody thought Doug could be a successful head coach in the league, and people who cover the NFL roundly dismissed his hiring. NFL.com famously ranked him as the worst coach in the league at one point—based largely on the fact that his pedigree was different from most other coaches'. Doug had never been a primary play caller before. However, those journalists said the same things about Andy Reid before the Eagles hired him, and that one worked out pretty well.

"Everybody thought I'd be a one and done," said Doug about his first season. He kept six assistants from the previous regime, including Jim Schwartz, who had been a head coach in the league. I think this continuity was really important. He hired Frank Reich, who has been highly successful. "I knew the type of play caller I was and that I wanted to be," Doug said.

> Doug instituted a player's council . . . and he really listened.

One of the earliest things Doug instituted was a player's council of leaders he trusted to provide feedback to his staff. And he really listened. Early on, we had a game where the play calling was unbalanced. A week later, Doug met with his council, and the play calling changed for the better. Best of all, nobody's feelings were hurt.

Doug leads the team. He's not trying to make anyone feel uncomfortable. No one is on the edge of their seats in each and every meeting. Doug does a great job of rewarding us with privileges and time off when we produce. That mentality definitely paid off during our magical 2017 season and the run we made through the playoffs that year.

CARSON WENTZ

We drafted Carson Wentz as the second overall pick in 2016, and he has been our guy. Even though we went 7–9 in 2016, there was a lot of optimism heading into the 2017 season. We knew we had a really talented team. We started hot, but then one of our better players was suspended for ten games, during which we went 2–8.

> We didn't really know how good we could be.

We went 13–3 through the regular season in 2017, won the NFC East, and secured our home field through the playoffs—all despite the fact that Carson tore his ACL in Week 14. My old friend Nick Foles, who has played a large role in this book, led us through the playoffs. We didn't really know how good we could be because we hadn't experienced a ton of team success.

Our first touchdown of the season, on the road against Washington, would be a harbinger of things to come. It featured Carson scrambling and avoiding pressure before bombing the ball downfield to Nelson Agholor. "He's an athletic kid," said our running back LeGarrette Blount about Carson. "He's a really special kid." That game, a win, ended with a Brandon Graham strip sack. Talk about foreshadowing!

We started off 1–1 and then went on a 9–1 stretch over the next 10 games. Kicker Jake Elliot hit a 61-yarder to give us the win over the Giants in Week 3. It seemed like nobody could stop us. We were going up 21–0 in the first quarter against good teams. Six times, we scored more than 30 points. And all the while, our confidence grew.

> Nobody had more fun than us during that stretch.

We played extremely fast in all three phases. Our offense would get a lead, and then our defense would hassle the other team's quarterback. Nobody had more fun than us during that stretch. We had an end zone celebration where Alshon Jeffrey would line us all up like bowling pins. He'd send an imaginary ball down the "lane," and we'd all fall over. Sometimes Blount danced with the cheerleaders—with pompoms! We had a blast playing the game.

DOMINATING CHICAGO

"It's in your hands," Doug said before our game against the Chicago Bears. If we won, we'd become the first ten-win team in the league that season.

"Our control. Right here in the palm of our hands. It's what we want. And this is where we make our run."

It was a perfectly clear, cool day in Philly. In the first quarter, I came off the line of scrimmage and kept expecting to be chipped by a defensive lineman or linebacker, but I ran free into the end zone, and Carson put the ball right on me. He ran to me so we could celebrate together. Then he made another great play in the second quarter when, feeling pressure, he spun out of the pocket and scrambled for almost 30 yards. Carson had the kind of innate feel you can't necessarily teach a quarterback—some guys are just born with it. That drive ended on a Nelson Agholor catch, run, and dive into the end zone.

By the time Carson hit former Bear Alshon Jeffrey in the end zone at the end of the second quarter, the game was basically over. We hung a dominant 31–3 win on them, and Carson was spectacular, passing for 227 yards and three scores.

THE RAMS—A SOMBER VICTORY

Our season took a dramatic turn in Week 14 against the Rams in Los Angeles—a game I missed due to injury. "We came out here for one reason, which is to take a championship and get back home," said Carson to the offense before the game. It would be a showdown between the NFL's two top picks in the 2016 draft—Carson and Rams quarterback Jared Goff. Both teams were angling for a playoff spot.

Carson threw three first-half touchdowns to put us up 21–7, including a dart to my great friend Trey Burton, who was playing in my spot. But Goff kept the Rams in it with a pair of touchdown passes, and their excellent special teams unit gave them the lead with a blocked punt leading to a score.

We were in a goal-line situation late in the third quarter with a pass play called. The play was pretty well covered by the Rams, and Carson started to scramble, as he often does. As he dove for the goal line, his legs were sandwiched in between two Ram defenders, Mark Barron and Morgan Fox. As soon as he got up, he knew something was wrong, but he stayed in the game. It's a testimony to his toughness that he rifled a touchdown pass to Alshon on the next play. What a tough dude!

It was unbelievable how our team rallied around Nick Foles. Even little things like center Jason Kelce pulling Nick over to the linemen and making sure everybody had a good feel for his cadence, which was a little different from Carson's, made a huge difference.

Our defense was great. In what would become a theme for us, a Chris Long strip sack led to a field goal, and a big third-down completion by Nick all but guaranteed victory. To top it off, Brandon Graham intercepted a pitch on the Rams' razzle-dazzle play. We were NFC East champs—but it was a somber locker room and a somber plane ride home.

"I won't lie, I shed a few tears when I got home that night," said quarterbacks coach Frank Reich. He meant it because of how much he respected Carson.

Carson met everybody on crutches in the locker room after the game. "We just won the NFC East. Let's go party!" he said. But we knew he was hurting. It would be Nick's show from that day forward, as Carson was out with a torn ACL.

"That's why I'm here," Nick said when asked if he was ready to lead the team. But people wrote us off immediately without Carson. They thought we were completely done.

"Nobody's giving us a chance, and that should piss you off," Doug told us. He was right. And it did.

FOLES TO THE RESCUE

Nick went out the next week and threw four touchdown passes against the Giants in a 34–29 victory—one of which was to me. But Nick struggled in our last two games, throwing for just 39 yards in a losing effort against the Cowboys in the season finale. We finished 13–3 on the year, but that wasn't our focus. As a team, we believed in Nick, and the stats didn't matter.

"I'm gonna play better, and I'm gonna be better than this in the play-offs," Nick said in a team meeting. I'd seen what he was capable of before, so I knew we were in good hands.

> As a team, we believed in Nick, and the stats didn't matter.

"Nick is a maniac in terms of wanting to throw the ball down the field," said Reich, and Doug did a great job of giving him a chance to do so. Doug studied Nick's tape so he could put our quarterback in the right play calls to get the job done and excel.

Home-field advantage in the playoffs is huge—especially in Philly, where we have the best home-field advantage in the league. Our fans are loud and ruthless. When we're rolling, the place is deafening.

Everything is magnified in the playoffs. In the beginning of the season, the guys are fresh and playing hard. In the middle, the overall feeling isn't as intense. But when the playoffs start, everybody's intensity ratchets up on *every* play of *every* game. It's a lot of fun. There are only four games during the first two weekends, and everybody watches them. I don't care about anything but winning—not even how many catches I get. The win is everything.

FENDING OFF THE FALCONS

We started with a home game in the divisional round against my old college teammate Levine Toilolo and the Atlanta Falcons. For the first time in history, a six seed (them) was favored over the top-seeded team (us). It was cold, which I think helped us and hurt them. LeGarrette Blount scored our only touchdown after fumbling a handoff from Nick earlier in the game.

Like a lot of other things, how those two players handled the situation was a microcosm of our season. Nobody freaked out—they just talked about it on the sideline and dealt with it. Blount calmly told Nick how he liked the handoffs, and they never had a problem again.

This game was a defensive struggle, and our defense came up huge in the end, stopping Atlanta from scoring four times on their final drive. On their last attempt, we broke up a pass intended for their star receiver, Julio Jones. That play was indicative of our team's mindset. The offense was relaxed on the sidelines because we knew our defense would come through. Sure enough, the pass rush got home, and the coverage was perfect. Incomplete pass. It was on to the NFC Championship Game!

After the Atlanta game, Chris Long and Lane Johnson introduced the "underdog masks" that became a fixture for our fans through the rest of the playoffs.

Carson's ability to show his colors during that time was huge. We knew he was struggling emotionally and wanted so badly to play, but he was also all in on Nick and our team. I always told him even when he wasn't playing that he was one of the *key* reasons we were successful. The confidence and the swagger our team had were built when he was playing. Everybody knew that.

Even when he was hurt, he was still showing up to the meetings, helping with the game plans, and talking with Nick and breaking down film. That's the sign of a real leader. Both men have their identities in Christ, and I think that showed through in how they treated and supported each other.

NFC CHAMPIONSHIP GAME—THE VIKINGS

Beating Atlanta meant that the Eagles were in the NFC Championship game for the first time in nine years. The Minnesota Vikings arrived because of a "miracle" play against the Saints in their divisional game. Both teams had a "team of destiny" type of narrative going in, and the Vikings were riding some momentum from a backup quarterback of their own, Case Keenum. Malcolm Jenkins, our safety, said before the game, "This is the last time we'll play together on this field, with this team. We're four quarters away from being legends—from being up there in those rafters where they can't take us down!"

We called a lot of run-pass options (RPOs) to keep their All-Pro safety Harrison Smith guessing and up near the line of scrimmage so we could hit passes down the seam behind him. The strategy worked.

We had a tough time stopping Latavius Murray and Kyle Rudolph early, and they drove down and scored on their first drive. "You have to weather the storm early in these games, because there are a lot of emotions on both sides," said Doug. "Once you ride that wave of emotion, it just becomes football after that."

Our pass rush started to get home, creating pressure that led to turnovers. Patrick Robinson took a pick-six to the house, and our crowd went crazy. Ronald Darby threw a huge block that allowed Patrick to get into the end zone.

The Vikings had another long, 11-play drive that ended in a strip sack by Derek Barnett, and it was all us from that point

> Even when he was hurt, Carson was still showing up to the meetings, helping with the game plans, and talking with Nick and breaking down film. That's the sign of a real leader.

forward. Chris Long recovered the fumble on a play that was emblematic of how General Manager Howie Roseman built our team through the draft (Barnett), with key veteran pickups along the way (Long).

Wide receiver Alshon Jeffrey, who scored right after the strip sack, was another one of those key veteran pickups—a big, physical receiver who can go up for balls and box people out. He was the weapon we'd needed all season. On that 53-yard play, Alshon saw Nick step up in the pocket and took off. Nick stood in the pocket for a *long* time despite the pressure and threw a *long* pass off-balance, which is a testament to his arm strength.

> "We lean on each other and we play for each other. Our guys didn't go out there and play in fear; we believed in each other."

"Everyone was locked in," said Nick afterward. "We lean on each other, and we play for each other. Our guys didn't go out there and play in fear; we believed in each other."

The Vikings had the best defense in the league, but we absolutely boat raced 'em. Everything we were calling was working. I even came up with a play on the sidelines—that's just how well everyone was seeing the game that day.

The coaches put a lot of trust in their players and are very receptive to us on the field as the games unfold. That speaks volumes to the culture Doug has created in Philadelphia. He has no ego and only wants to call the best plays. That mind-set carried over onto the biggest stage with the Philly Special.

I ran a corner route early in the game, and I knew that Vikings safety Harrison Smith had his eyes on the quarterback. I knew if we ran an out and up, we would make a huge play. Then we ran it again and went for 40 yards. It's just one of those things when you're in the zone. I have amazingly receptive coaches, and there's a ton of trust, which is unusual in most football contexts.

UNFINISHED BUSINESS

After the NFC Championship Game, Doug said, "We have some unfinished business. We're gonna pack our bags and head to Minneapolis." In a really cool, classy moment after the game, Case Keenum gave Nick Foles a huge hug and said, "Nobody deserves this more than you." That's a part of NFL life that most people don't see. There are a lot of great guys in this league.

Julie wasn't able to be there that night, which was tough because everybody else had their wives and girlfriends down on the field. I hung out with myself and took it all in. There was so much joy. There was confetti coming down, and everybody was going crazy. I FaceTimed Julie the moment I got into the locker room, and she cried when I told her we were going to the Super Bowl. She was in San Diego playing for the US Women's National Soccer Team against Denmark, a game in which she scored the winning goal.

> There are a lot of great guys in this league.

My mom goes to every home game, so I wasn't going home to an empty condo, but I couldn't wait for Julie to be there with me at the Super Bowl.

SUPER BOWL CIRCUS

I thought Doug did a fantastic job preparing for the Super Bowl. On Wednesday, just like a normal week, we went over the basic game plan. On Thursday, we focused on third-down plays. On Friday, we went over red-zone plays. Nick played phenomenal football that week in practice, which allowed him to gain confidence. Our offense also got comfortable running our staple plays with Nick at quarterback.

> Doug even simulated the long Super Bowl halftime for us.

Doug even simulated the long Super Bowl halftime for us. In the middle of practice, after a couple of periods, we went to the locker room for 30 minutes. Some guys would lie down. Others would take a shower and put on fresh gear for the second half. The idea was to experience a total shutdown and restart. Then we went through another dynamic warm-up after "halftime."

The New England Patriots head coach Bill Belichick talked about doing the same thing. "It really gets into a whole restarting mentality," he said during an interview. "It's not like taking a break and coming out in the second half. It's like starting the game all over again. It's like playing a game, stopping, and then playing a second game."

SUPER BOWL WEEK

There's a lot that can take away from the game itself during Super Bowl week. On opening night, the team sat on a podium and got drilled by the media. Some of the guys really got into it. My old draft-class buddy Lane Johnson is a natural star and wore running back Jay Ajayi's sunglasses. He talked about the dog masks that Eagles fans in Philly were wearing because we had been the underdogs in our playoff games. "I think it's created a lot of energy for us and helped us out as a team," Lane said.

> Michael Irvin asked me who the best athlete was in our house. I answered that question like I always answer it: Julie.

"It's about the journey, and it's about the men I've done it with," Nick said.

"This is who I am . . . this is my personality," said Doug on why he was so calm—in contrast to Bill Belichick. "I tell my players to let their personalities show, and I've gotta do the same thing. You gotta enjoy the moment because you never know when you're gonna be back."

Doug had played in a Super Bowl 20 years prior as a member of the Green Bay Packers and a backup to Brett Favre.

A surreal moment for me came when Hall of Fame wide receiver Michael Irvin asked me who the best athlete was in my house. I answered that question like I always answer it: Julie. It was amazing to be able to enjoy that moment with her. She was at opening night in a vintage Eagles sweater that looked like it came from Reggie White's era. She was working for US Soccer as a member of the media. The highlight was being able to do a one-on-one interview with my wife.

> For every game, I get up and go to the hotel lobby to have the same breakfast: chocolate chip waffles; eggs with spinach, cheese, mushrooms, and onions; and hash browns.

The team did the same thing on Wednesday and Thursday. By the time we got to the game, it was almost a relief. "There is a game sometime tonight, right?" Doug joked with a referee during warm-ups. We were all feeling ready to get out there and play football.

THE DAY OF THE GAME

We were literally locked in the team hotel. There were armored cars in the streets. We couldn't go out in Minnesota because everybody would know who we were. Even so, we tried to make the day of the game as normal as possible, and as such, I stuck to my usual pregame routine.

> A game day is just another chance to go out and have fun with my teammates and try to glorify Christ.

For every game, I get up and go to the hotel lobby to have the same breakfast: chocolate chip waffles; eggs with spinach, cheese, mushrooms, and onions; and hash browns. Then I go back up to the room to get dressed. I always wear a suit to the game. The suit is a symbol: it's a workday—time to go to the office. While I'm changing, I call my pastor. We have a two-minute discussion, we pray for the day, and he prays over me. As I'm driving to the stadium, I'll FaceTime Julie just to check in one last time. She always says, "Go dominate and I love you."

As an added bonus, since the Super Bowl was an afternoon game, our pastor came and led church that morning. He spoke on Judges 7 with Gideon and the Midianites.

I'm typically at the stadium three hours before the game. I get an IV for hydration and listen to worship music to try to set my body and spirit right. Then I foam roll my legs, stretch, and activate my body. Next, I go out with the quarterbacks, tight ends, and wide receivers and run some routes on air. Then I go through a catch routine with my third-string quarterback. After that, I go over blocking fundamentals with my coach just to make sure—one more time—everything is ready to go.

Finally, I change into my uniform and go out for full team warm-ups. This step really hit me on Super Bowl Sunday—pulling on the Eagles jersey with the Super Bowl patch on the shoulder. I'm usually extremely relaxed on game days and never really get too anxious about anything. The pressure of the game has subsided as I get further into my walk with Christ. A game day is just another chance to go out and have fun with my teammates and try to glorify Him.

The first warm-up at the Super Bowl is when it all hit me. I stepped out under the lights at the Vikings' stadium and saw all the media outlets with their TV setups. I knew then it was definitely a different environment.

"Do what you've done all year," said Doug. "Let it all out."

Carson gave Nick a big hug before the game and said, "Enjoy this. *Enjoy this day!*" It was so classy, and again, I truly believe that doesn't happen for either guy apart from Christ.

THE PHILLY SPECIAL

Going into the game, I knew there was a good chance I was going to be double-teamed on third downs and in the red zone. Belichick tends to zero in on one option and completely take it away. I also knew it wouldn't ruin the play if I was doubled. Doug and the staff did a great job of preparing me mentally for the game. Early on, I didn't get the ball a lot, but then Alshon Jeffrey and Nelson Agholor started going off. They had big games.

> The game produced more than 1,150 yards of total offense—the most in any NFL game.

In fact, the game produced more than 1,150 yards of total offense—the most in any NFL game ever. With the game tied at 3–3 in the first quarter, Nick threw the kind of high, arching 50-50 ball that Alshon has made a living on during his NFL career. He caught it in the end zone to put us up 10–3. Former Patriot LeGarrette Blount got into the action next on a long scoring run. But the Pats were no easy out—a Stephen Gostkowski field goal and a James White touchdown kept them in the game.

Possibly the most famous play of Super Bowl LII took place near the end of the second quarter. It involved Corey Clement, Trey Burton, and Nick Foles on fourth down and goal at the one yard line.

"We're going for it right here," said Doug through the headset to Nick.

"You want Philly Philly?" Nick asked from near the sideline.

Doug agreed, and it was the shortest play call in NFL history: "Philly Special."

On the play, Nick moved up behind the offensive line, and the ball was snapped to running back Corey Clement. Corey went on to pitch the ball to my great friend Trey Burton (who, as you recall, was freakishly athletic), who passed the ball to a wide-open Nick to score a touchdown. In scoring, Nick became the first player in Super Bowl history to both throw and catch a touchdown. I was blocking a Patriots linebacker right in front of where Nick caught the ball in the end zone, so I had a perfect view of his catch, which was awesome.

It was described by NFL Films as "a play that the Eagles had never called before, run on fourth down by an undrafted rookie running back pitching the football to a third-string tight end who had never attempted an NFL pass before, throwing to a backup quarterback who had never caught an NFL or college pass before, [pulled off] on the biggest stage for football."

That one play proves how much faith Doug has in his players. It also shows the level of courage he has to try something new in a situation where other coaches would go with the "safe" call and play the percentages. That's why Doug is such a special coach and the Eagles are such a special organization. The talent we amassed as a team, through unconventional channels, really got to shine on the Philly Special.

"Foles, why were you so open?" asked Trey on the sideline.

"I sold it," Nick replied.

And he had. After the snap, Nick just stood there watching Corey like it was a run play to the opposite side. Then he leaked out into the end zone, where he was all alone.

"You've got more catches than Tom [Brady]," said one of our trainers. Brady had dropped one on a trick play earlier in the game.

"We've got good answers for everything," I said to Nick on the sideline in the fourth quarter. "They cannot stop us."

The Super Bowl gave me a chance to play against one of the NFL's great tight ends—Rob Gronkowski. He's a freak—a beast—with his bionic elbow brace and huge hands. Gronk was quiet in the first half, but the Pats came out slinging it to him in the third quarter. Gronk scored to cut our lead to 22–19. He got us again in the fourth quarter on a corner route to put them up by a point.

"We've got good answers for everything," I said to Nick on the sideline in the fourth quarter. "They cannot stop us."

TOUCHDOWN MENTALITY

The end of the drive is what many people remember; however, Doug's decision to go for it on fourth and one at midfield only reinforced the trust he had in his team. We called a staple play where we run a bunch of crossing routes, hoping to run interference on each other. Wily veteran Brent Celek did a great job on the guy covering me. Nick sidestepped the pass rusher and threw the ball to me right at the sticks.

When the ball is in the air, you can feel where the defenders are, so I knew I was going to get hit the moment the ball arrived, but all I cared about was getting that first down. I told myself, "Whatever it takes!" I caught the ball, reached out past the marker, and the ref signaled first down! We were rolling, and we weren't going to look back. Our mentality on that last drive was touchdown all the way.

Our staff did a great job of scheming me out of the double-team by sending Corey Clement in motion and leaving me in isolation against a Pro Bowl safety. I was alone in single coverage, out wide at the top of the formation. We had a slant on, and Nick put out a great throw. I was able to catch the ball, take three steps, and dive into the end zone.

> You just hate to give a quarterback like Tom Brady the ball with any time left on the clock.

The refs reviewed the play for a long time because I bobbled the ball when I hit the ground in the end zone. They were trying to determine whether I was a runner and had made a "football move" after the catch. Trey Burton and I were on the field talking as they were going over the replay. We knew that the whole city of Philly was going to go crazy if the refs overturned it. They finally called a touchdown, much to the chagrin of Chris Collinsworth.

At that time, I didn't think I had just caught the game-winning touchdown. I truly believed we would have to go out and score again based on the way the Patriots were rolling. You just hate to give a quarterback like Tom Brady the ball with any time left on the clock.

Brent Celek slapped me on the shoulder and screamed, "Ahhh, my man!" while safety Malcolm Jenkins reminded us, "Somebody on the defense is about to be a hero."

That hero would turn out to be defensive end Brandon Graham, who would strip sack Brady—a fellow Michigan alum—to seal the game.

GIDEON AND THE MIDIANITES

I felt like God was all over our season that year. It felt a lot like the account of Gideon leading Israel into battle against the Midianites in Judges. The Lord talks to Gideon before the battle and explains that he has too many soldiers.

The Lord feared that Israel would boast of its own military might and not give glory to Him if they went into battle. So God whittled the number down from 22,000 soldiers to 10,000. But even then, God said, "That's too many," so He downsized the army again—this time by observing the way the soldiers drank the water at the side of the river.

With the 300 men who lapped the water out of their hands, God said He would deliver the nation of Israel, and He did so in a way that left *no doubt* that it was the hand of the Lord that delivered them.

> So the people took provisions in their hands, and their trumpets. And he sent all the rest of Israel every man to his tent, but retained the 300 men. And the camp of Midian was below him in the valley.
>
> That same night the LORD said to him, "Arise, go down against the camp, for I have given it into your hand. But if you are afraid to go down, go down to the camp with Purah your servant. And you shall hear what they say, and afterward your hands shall be strengthened to go down against the camp." Then he went down with Purah his servant to the outposts of the armed men who were in the camp. And the Midianites and the Amalekites and all the people of the East lay along the valley like locusts in abundance, and their camels were without number, as the sand that is on the seashore in abundance (Judges 7:8-12).

Finally, the Lord delivered victory to Gideon and his army:

> So Gideon and the hundred men who were with him came to the outskirts of the camp at the beginning of the middle watch, when they had just set the watch. And they blew the trumpets and smashed the jars that were in their hands. Then the three companies blew the trumpets and broke the jars. They held in their left hands the torches, and in their right hands the trumpets to blow. And they cried out, "A sword for the LORD and for Gideon!" Every man stood in his place around the camp, and all the army ran. They cried out and fled. When they blew the 300 trumpets, the LORD set every man's sword against his comrade and against all the army. And the army fled as far as Beth-shittah toward Zererah, as far as the border of Abel-meholah, by Tabbath. And the men of Israel were called out from Naphtali and from Asher and from all Manasseh, and they pursued after Midian.
>
> Gideon sent messengers throughout all the hill country of Ephraim, saying, "Come down against the Midianites and capture the waters against them, as far as Beth-barah, and also the Jordan." So all the men of Ephraim were called out, and they captured the waters as far as Beth-barah, and also the Jordan. And they captured the two princes of Midian, Oreb and Zeeb. They killed Oreb at the rock of Oreb, and Zeeb they killed at the winepress of Zeeb. Then they pursued Midian, and they brought the heads of Oreb and Zeeb to Gideon across the Jordan (Judges 7:19-25).

I felt like that was our season. Looking at our team from the outside, we had so much talent go down—a potentially Hall of Fame left tackle, a star quarterback, arguably a Hall of Fame running back, and a star linebacker. If we'd had all those guys, we might not have seen God in our victory. But with all of those things stacked against us, and given how we came together and loved each other through it, God received glory.

On the podium after the game, our head coach said, "I just want to thank our Lord and Savior Jesus Christ." Nick and I did the same thing. I don't mean to say that God was a rabbit's foot or that He even cares who wins a football game—but I think the adversity we faced was a way to glorify God. I felt like He was so good and so alive.

"Love just means you care for each other unconditionally, you have no hidden agenda, and that you genuinely want what's best for the person next to you," said Nick. That statement really encapsulates that whole season and how I feel about our team in general.

> Because of Christ, I felt free to fully enjoy the moment while knowing it wasn't the end-all, be-all of my existence.

It took me a week to get back to everyone who reached out to me after the game as the calls and texts came rolling in. They were extremely supportive, and I didn't feel overwhelmed. Because of Christ, I felt free to fully enjoy the moment while knowing it wasn't the end-all, be-all of my existence.

It was great to be able to hang out with my wife and my family after the game. And it was a blast to be able to hang out with my Eagles brothers at our postgame party. The year was so tough, and the season was so long. I had worked my whole life for that moment, and it had finally arrived.

10

HOW FIRM A
FOUNDATION

My mind-set going into the 2018 season was to continue to improve as an individual. My motivation is to be one of the best tight ends to ever play and to glorify God through it all. Having the mentality to be better than the previous year, I attacked the off-season and focused on my weaknesses.

"There's gotta be some time in your life when pain has taught you something," said Head Coach Doug Pederson after an early season loss. "When defeat has taught you something. It hurt. It stung. It made you better as a team and as a family."

He was right. Many coaches say a lot of things to milk wins out of their players, but I could tell by the sincerity on Doug's face that he meant every word and he cared about us as men. His authenticity really resonates with the team. He understands the struggles and the highs and lows of the game.

Doug is not your typical authoritarian figure. As players, we're not afraid that he's going to call us out. He treats us like professionals. He gives us the freedom to police ourselves, and we don't want to disappoint him. He's never going to panic. There's never going to be an ounce of doubt or a moment when his confidence is shaken. It's about us—the team—and what we're doing. We control the situation, and we don't worry about what other people are saying or doing.

"What are you willing to give up to go the rest of the way?" he asked us eight difficult games into the 2018 season. "Are you willing to sacrifice yourself for your team?"

CARSON'S RETURN AGAINST THE COLTS

We dealt with a lot of adversity in the 2018 season. We were the defending Super Bowl champions, and that put a target on our back. Our quarterback Carson Wentz got injured again, and our defense was depleted by injuries.

> "Way to battle, brother. I love you," I said to him after the game. "Love you too," he replied.

NFL Films had me mic'd up in Week 3 for Carson's return against the Colts in Philly. It was a matchup against my old college friend and teammate Andrew Luck, and it was a lot of fun. I was recorded screaming things like "Let's *go*!" to Carson and encouraging my teammates along the way. "That's the first of many," I said to rookie tight end Dallas Goedert after he scored his first NFL touchdown. I believe we have the best tight end room in the league, and we have five guys in there who could be NFL starters.

"Good hit; I like that," I said to Colts safety Malik Hooker after he rocked me along the sidelines on one catch. "You're a really good player."

I got a chance to contribute as a run blocker in the fourth quarter when Wendell Smallwood put us on top. I had a double-team on with our left tackle, and Wendell was able to run right behind us into the end zone.

We sacked Andrew on a fourth and goal to seal the game, and Andrew pounded the ground repeatedly in frustration. He's the ultimate competitor, and I know it killed him to lose like that.

"Way to battle, brother. I love you," I said to him after the game.

"Love you too," he replied.

In Week 11, when we lost 48–7 against New Orleans, I didn't even know most of the guys who were on the field for us on defense. Our team was so run down, the general manager was signing players off the street, bringing them into the facility for a crash course, and then putting them on the field.

"This game is not gonna define the Philadelphia Eagles and the rest of our season," Doug said afterward. "It is going to refine us. It's gonna make us sharper. I have too much confidence in this group here—way too much confidence."

Our season started in earnest with that speech.

REFINED AGAINST THE REDSKINS

We went 1–0 the next week and then 1–0 the week after that. I was mic'd up again in a Monday night game against the Redskins in Week 12. Doug moved me around the formation a lot. I was lined out wide, in line as a traditional tight end, and involved in some run-pass options (RPOs) and play-action passes.

My old friend Mark Sanchez started for the Redskins because of injuries they'd had at the position. Still, we made the game closer than we should have. Their ageless running back Adrian Peterson went 90 yards to the house, prompting me to say simply, "Oh boy."

"Welcome back, brother," I said to Darren Sproles after his touchdown run.

> Later in the game, I was able to break the Eagles' all-time record for receptions in a season, which was held by Brian Westbrook.

We had an ageless running back of our own, and he wasn't going to be stopped. Later in the game, I was able to break the Eagles' all-time record for receptions in a season, which was held by Brian Westbrook.

We won 28–13. I had nine catches, which was a lot of fun. When we came out for our victory formation, I congratulated Josh Norman and Ryan Kerrigan from the Redskins, saying, "I gotta get both y'all's jerseys someday!" I gave their physical safety D.J. Swearinger a hug and said how much I loved playing against him.

Needless to say, we needed some help to get into the playoffs, but in winning five games in six weeks, we did our part.

"Congratulations on being in the postseason," Doug said. "It's been a grind, but you know what, you enjoy the journey!" It's rare to hear a coach speak in those terms. In the NFL, most coaches have a grim sense of duty, and there is little talk of joy. Doug seemed to remember that we were playing a game.

BATTLING THE BEARS

In our first playoff game in Chicago, we battled against the Bears. Soldier Field, like Philly, is a tough place to play in December because it's cold and windy, and their fan base is loud and aggressive. We gave a great team effort in all three phases, but we had trouble putting the ball in the end zone. Our defense and special teams kept us in it.

> In the NFL, most coaches have a grim sense of duty, and there is little talk of joy. Doug seemed to remember that we were playing a game.

The Bears were up 15–10 in the fourth quarter. We put together a huge offensive drive with less than two minutes left in the game, and I was able to make a big fingertip catch to keep the drive moving.

We got the ball with first and goal inside the five, and they stopped our first two running plays to Darren Sproles.

On third and goal, they broke up a pass intended for Alshon Jeffrey. Finally, on fourth and goal from the two, Nick found trade acquisition Golden Tate just over the goal line for the go-ahead score, prompting announcer Chris Collinsworth to declare, "The trade was officially worth it." The Bears stopped our two-point conversion play, so we went up by a point with about a minute to go.

They got a good kick return from Tarik Cohen and made a couple of plays to get in field goal range. They would have won the game, but their kicker hit the upright with five seconds remaining. With a kneel down, we were headed to New Orleans and the divisional round of the playoffs.

THE END OF A SPECIAL YEAR

We were ecstatic to have another opportunity to go into New Orleans, where we'd previously gotten our butts kicked in Week 11. We intercepted Drew Brees on the first play of the game, and then Nick Foles hit Jordan Matthews in the end zone on the ensuing drive. We went up 14–0 on a quarterback sneak, at which point you could hear a pin drop in the normally loud Superdome.

Unfortunately, that was about it for us offensively, and Brees started doing his thing for New Orleans—which is to say, we saw a lot of Michael Thomas catching passes. Their running back Mark Ingram had a couple of long, backbreaking runs. We lost 20–14. We came close but couldn't get it done.

The game ended on an interception that went through the hands of Alshon Jeffrey. Afterward, I found Nick and said, "We did all we could. I love you, man. I love playing with you."

A key characteristic of this team is the resiliency we showed week in and

> I found Nick and said, "We did all we could. I love you, man. I love playing with you."

week out—in victory or defeat. Nothing came easy for us in the 2018 season. We had to battle for each and every yard. I ended the season with 116 receptions, 1,163 yards, and 8 touchdowns and was able to break Jason Witten's record for receptions by a tight end in a season.

It was a really special year for me individually, but I still have a lot to improve on. Still, no matter who's covering me, I always feel like I have some kind of advantage—that I'm going to be open. I feel like all great players have that mentality.

IN THE NFL, CHANGE IS THE ONLY CONSTANT

I'm thinking a lot about relationships as I write this morning. I'm coming off another long, savage lift and thinking about Nick Foles, who is about to sign a contract with the Jacksonville Jaguars. It'll be a great opportunity for Nick, who deserves to start somewhere, but it's a tough reminder of how often I have to say goodbye to people in this business.

Injuries and goodbyes are the toughest things about being an NFL player. But at the same time, I found out that my old teammate DeSean Jackson is returning to the Eagles via a trade. Anything can happen in the NFL, and change is the only constant.

I've been blessed to have had great teammates and great friends over the years, which I think is increasingly rare in the NFL. This free-agency period has illustrated the role of social media in our lives. Guys are announcing their deals on Twitter, and players are courting other players via their Instagram accounts. A guy who isn't a star in the league can become a household name because of his online interactions with fans.

I think social media has made a lot of people extremely cautious of their actions. It's not even worth me going out to a club (which is not something I do a lot of anyway). But if someone takes a picture of me at a club, it's assumed that I'm not giving 100 percent to my team or to Julie. Guys are a lot more introverted as a result. They spend a lot less time going out because they're constantly being scrutinized.

I think it's important for people to remember that social media offers only surface-level interaction. Now if you post a picture and don't get the likes and comments you expect, you might think, "Is there something wrong with me? People don't like me." There's also a misconception right now that males cannot be vulnerable with each other. As a result, we move through life in these very shallow interactions, which mostly occur online.

I'm also thinking a lot about Julie, who is off in the midst of her pro soccer season. A verse from 1 John is central to our lives: "We love because he first loved us" (4:19). We got matching tattoos of the verse on Valentine's Day. I loved going to get that with her—and even loved the gentle pain of the tattoo needle going in and out of my skin. I love the permanence. I love that it's a constant reminder of Christ's love for me and the bond Julie and I share in Christ.

> Injuries and goodbyes are the toughest things about being an NFL player.

I got my first tattoo when I was 16. It says "Family First 4," and my brothers all have the same ink. When I was going through that hard time, the tattoo was a place to put all the stress and anger I couldn't communicate in any other way. Any new tattoos I get— like the cross I have on my finger—are much more meaningful, and they serve as reminders that I can't change anyone's life in a positive way apart from Christ.

THE ERTZ FAMILY FOUNDATION

Having a charitable foundation was something Julie and I always had on our hearts, but we never felt confident about running it, and we never felt a real push to get it started. But Carson Wentz goes down to Haiti every year, and he recently invited me to come along. He met his wife there, so Haiti has a special place in his heart. I decided last year that nothing was going to hold me back.

> Mission of Hope distributes almost 300,000 meals a week. They run orphanages and schools. They are on the ground every day changing Haiti. It opened my eyes.

In Haiti, we worked with Mission of Hope, which aims to "transform every man, woman, and child on Haiti through the love of Jesus Christ." To go there and see a foundation backed by Christ was amazing. Mission of Hope distributes almost 300,000 meals a week. They run orphanages and schools. They are on the ground every day changing Haiti. It opened my eyes.

LOVE, JOY, AND BEAUTY

In Haiti, there were no paved roads, and trash was everywhere. Then I met the people, and it was amazing. The community. The love. The joy in their situation was so apparent and so mind-blowing to me. I wanted to dig deeper.

We played soccer with a group of kids at a field that I wouldn't have touched when I was growing up. If I saw even the smallest hole, I would have said, "I can't train there. What if I roll my ankle?" In Haiti, there were rocks, dirt, string hanging from the backs of the goals, and only tiny patches of grass. The kids didn't even have a ball—they used an empty water bottle. But they played so hard and had so much fun diving on the ground and attempting bicycle kicks. I saw their athleticism and could just imagine what they could accomplish if they had the proper training.

I went into their village and saw the problems and the trials they face every day. They have to walk a mile for clean water. If you look at the water, you can actually see the bacteria forming in it. My skin crawled thinking about it.

We painted a little concrete house while we were there. The people were so appreciative, and they took so much pride in making it the prettiest house they could. There was no envy or jealousy in their community.

> Then I met the people, and it was amazing. The community. The love. The joy in their situation was so apparent and so mind-blowing to me. I wanted to dig deeper.

The thing that resonated with me from the trip—even more than the natural beauty of the Caribbean—was the people. They don't have many material things, but they find so much joy and love in their community. It was powerful to me. I fell in love with the people I met there and wanted to share their perspective on life.

THE LAUNCH

I came back from Haiti and told Julie, "I think it's time to start a foundation." We started the Ertz Family Foundation in May 2018 with a focus on sports and educational opportunities for kids in Haiti, the Bay Area, and Philly.

We held a formal launch event at the stadium in Philadelphia and were truly touched by the outpouring of support from friends, family, and people in the sports community. The lower concourse of the stadium was decked out with tables of food and our logo, and we heard from a variety of great speakers, including former NBA legend David Robinson.

> We're going to do as much as is humanly possible to share the love in a city that has shared so much love with us.

We were joined by some incredible corporate sponsors that night, including the Eagles Charitable Foundation, the Philadelphia 76ers, the *Philadelphia Enquirer*, and Campbell's Soups.

"We know that Zach and I aren't going to have these platforms forever," said Julie at the event. We both want to be good stewards of where God has us and what He's blessed us with today. We're going to do as much as is humanly possible to share the love in a city that has shared so much love with us.

HELPING THE BEST WE CAN

We've held a lot of events to raise money. We started a scholarship fund in Haiti, where less than 1 percent of students receive any kind of higher education, to send kids to college. We've been able to fund 16 scholarships so far. They provide for room and board, tuition, meals, and learning materials at colleges and universities in Haiti to orphaned teenagers from the Mission of Hope: Haiti orphanage.

We've hired a full-time high school counselor in the Bay Area. Julie and I were both fortunate to be able to go to amazing colleges and had many advantages growing up in the athletic realm. There is a huge gap between the haves and have-nots in terms of athletic and educational opportunities, and we hope that our foundation can be a bridge between those two groups.

In 2018, we had the chance to give a $10,000 grant (matched by the Eagles) to a high school football team in Philly. A homeless man had squatted in their equipment shed and had gradually sold all their football equipment. My mom tipped me off about the story, and then we got the Eagles involved. The donations included 45 game jerseys, 47 pairs of Eagles practice pants, 60 pairs of socks, 15 footballs, 1 two-man sled, 1 tackle tube, linemen chutes, 2 Gatorade coolers, and of course, a new storage unit with a lock.

During the 2018 season, the Ertz Family Foundation launched a charitable campaign with Chegg, an education tech company. Chegg donated $1,086 to the foundation for every touchdown I scored and $860 for every first down.

The foundation has been a huge success thus far. The best part is that it's something Julie and I do together, and it's been great to see her heart in this. I didn't think it was humanly possible to feel closer to her, but running a foundation together has done that.

Time management has been a huge challenge. During football season, I just want to focus on the game. I love doing the other stuff, but football is what allows me to do that other stuff. Having to learn to be patient and hear everyone out has stretched me in unique nonfootball ways. Julie and I want to change people's lives in the city, and there's a lot of thought that goes into our mission.

> There is a huge gap between the haves and have-nots in terms of athletic and educational opportunities, and we hope that our foundation can be a bridge between those two groups.

> I didn't think it was humanly possible to feel closer to her, but running a foundation together has done that.

My mom runs the foundation. She's been an executive director for two previous nonprofits, so she knows all about it. I talk to my pastor frequently so we can keep Christ at the center of what we're doing. Lord willing, we'll have the opportunity to share the joy of sports and higher education with others in Haiti, Philly, and the Bay Area. For more information and to find out how to get involved, visit ertzfamilyfoundation.org.

BEING VULNERABLE

Playing in the NFL is definitely a fun job to have. It's the culmination of a dream. At the same time, it is a job—one that comes with a lot of stress. You're judged on what you've done to help your team win a game. That thought drives me even today in the off-season. The most fun and gratifying part of the job is being able to be vulnerable with 53 other men who share this physically demanding profession.

> My brothers in Christ were on an even keel whether they had good or bad days. I was envious of that.

NFL players are pulled in a million different directions all the time. Having brothers in Christ to whom I grow closer every day is what helps me the most in my walk with Christ. It's what makes the NFL fun for me—the relationships that thrive in this competitive environment.

As I mentioned, in 2016, I failed to block Vontaze Burfict, and my life changed forever. That play led to me fully committing and surrendering my life to Christ. My teammates being there for me was a huge factor that the Lord used to draw me to Himself.

Before the Burfict thing, I was ego-centric and me-centric and wanted the ball all the time. I was so living and dying with football. Trying to protect myself. My feeling right after the Burfict play was, "I'm done with football. Done trying to find my worth in football."

Football was always a thing I felt like I controlled. After that I just submitted everything. I said, "Jesus, I'm done. I submit everything to You." My brothers in Christ helped with that. They were on an even keel whether they had a good or bad day. I was envious of that.

That play was the best thing that ever happened to me.

LIVING AS DISCIPLES

I took the first steps of my faith walk with my teammate Trey Burton, another tight end. His identity was in Christ. I saw his walk every day in the way he lived. After I decided to submit my life to Christ, he asked, "Why don't we just start reading a chapter a night in the book of John?" Trey was able to talk about my new faith in a nonjudgmental way. He planted seeds in my ear during every practice, meeting, and game we shared, but his actions really shaped my view.

> Jesus is the best therapist . . . but sometimes it's best to have somebody who can slap you straight.

He took time out of his schedule to disciple me in our building, where the focus is always on football. That played a huge role in me walking with the Lord today. He reframed my mind to get me focused on growing in my walk. Once I committed everything to Jesus, we started coming to the facility early so we could watch game film while we ate breakfast and then study the book of John. Those times were really powerful.

It was tough for me when Trey left the Eagles for a starting job with the Chicago Bears, but nobody deserved it more. I used to joke that he was my therapist. He was the guy I could talk to. He was a groomsman in my wedding. With him not being there, 2018 was extremely difficult. Jesus is the best therapist, but sometimes it's nice to have somebody who can slap you straight.

So as I come to the end of this book journey, I'm reminded that there are still guys on the Eagles who can fill that role in my life, and now I can fill that role in the lives of other young guys. As I type this, my quarterback, Carson Wentz, is in Israel walking where Jesus walked. I can't wait to hear his stories when he comes back, and I can't wait to go there with Julie someday.

A LIGHT IN PHILADELPHIA

It's easy for me to go dark and shut everything out when I focus on football. But to do that is to not make the most of this platform. I'm trying to build the kingdom and be light in Philadelphia. We're still trying to grow as believers on our team. On Thursday, we hold a Bible study in the building with our team chaplain, Pastor Ted. Saturday night before the game, we'll all get together for prayer and fellowship and a study of Romans.

> Playing in this city and meeting the guys in this locker room has changed my life in so many ways.

The guys truly care about one another. We are all invested in our teammates' success, which is something you don't often find in this business. That said, there's a good chance that a lot of my closest friends on the team aren't going to be here next year. I've already said goodbye to Nick Foles and Trey Burton. Jordan Hicks just signed with the Arizona Cardinals. That's the reality of this business and the toughest thing about this league. But I'll always feel that playing in this city and meeting the guys in this locker room have changed my life in so many ways.

I'm forever indebted and grateful for the chance to play for Doug Pederson. He's helped me through so many things—on and off the field. He's an amazing coach and an amazing person. I love playing here, and I never take it for granted.

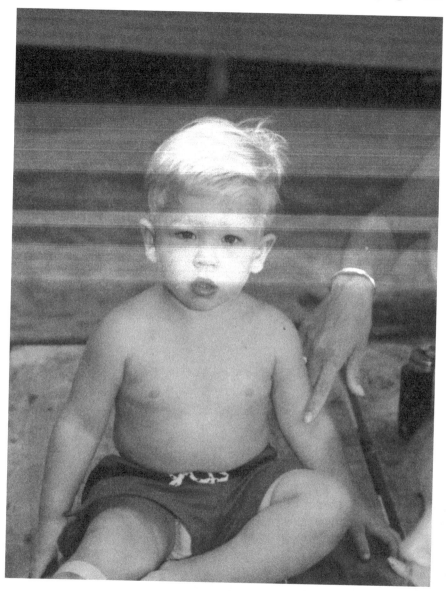

A toddler and already jacked.

Enjoying Halloween with my brothers, "Boomer Esiason" and "Troy Aikman."
My last days in a 49ers uniform and affiliating with the Cowboys!

Ready to become the next Jordan . . .
as soon as I get this finger out of my ear.

Family has always come first for me—even back in the day!

My hair in all its Adam Morrison glory.

Just leaning casually against some rocks, with a football
in hand, next to some flowers. As one does.

I do it all for these folks. I wouldn't have done a fraction of
what I've done without my mom and my brothers.

Monte Vista High School basketball. We won a lot of games together!

Hauling one in at Stanford in the Big Game.

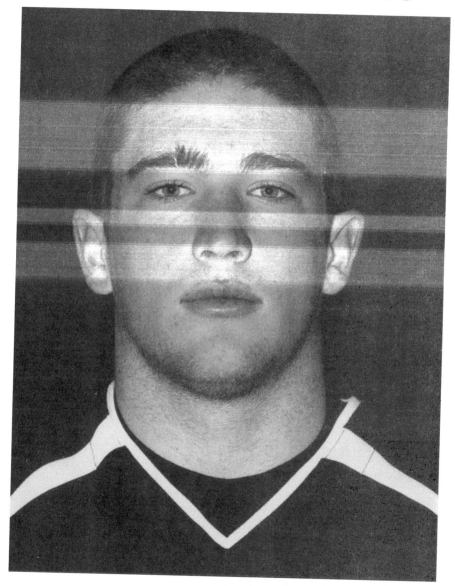

This, kids, is how you do "football neck" when photographed.
Coming soon to a "Wanted" poster near you.

Diving for extra yardage in the Fiesta Bowl.

To learn more about Harvest House books and
to read sample chapters, visit our website:

www.harvesthousepublishers.com

HARVEST HOUSE PUBLISHERS
EUGENE, OREGON